Josh Clark

DESIGNING FOR TOUCH

Responsible Responsive Design
Scott Jehl

You're My Favorite Client
Mike Monteiro

On Web Typography
Jason Santa Maria

Sass for Web Designers
Dan Cederholm

Just Enough Research
Erika Hall

Content Strategy for Mobile
Karen McGrane

Design Is a Job
Mike Monteiro

Mobile First
Luke Wroblewski

Designing for Emotion
Aarron Walter

Responsive Web Design
Ethan Marcotte

The Elements of Content Strategy
Erin Kissane

Visit abookapart.com for our full list of titles.

Publisher: Jeffrey Zeldman
Designer: Jason Santa Maria
Executive Director: Katel LeDû
Editor: Tina Lee
Copyeditor: Caren Litherland
Proofreader: Sally Kerrigan
Compositor: Rob Weychert
Ebook Producer: Ron Bilodeau

ISBN: 978-1-9375572-8-7

A Book Apart
New York, New York
http://abookapart.com

10 9 8 7 6 5 4 3 2 1

TABLE OF CONTENTS

For Team Awesome

AND JUST LIKE THAT, the floodgates opened, releasing a seemingly endless torrent of different-sized glass rectangles on an unsuspecting public. We, the designers of the world, had no choice but to flail our arms in an effort to keep our heads above the waterline of this new sea of devices.

But swim we did, as we slowly but surely began to make sense of this new mobile medium. Native designers sank their teeth in and explored the unique capabilities of these devices, creating experiences that pushed the medium into even more amazing territory. And on the web front, we witnessed the rise of responsive design, which allowed designers to reflow layouts so they looked and functioned beautifully on any device, irrespective of screen size. Nowadays, squishy sites abound on the world wide web, and designers have an arsenal of tools to ensure their layouts work on phones, tablets, and everything in between. Mission accomplished, right?

If only it were that simple. You see, reflowing layout is one piece of this giant multi-device design puzzle. We also interact with our newly squishy interfaces with these clumsy sausages we call fingers. This forces our hand (har har) as designers to ensure our user interfaces aren't just viewable on different-sized screens, but are also finger friendly.

Ergonomics, posture, context, and the tactile nature of touch all have real ramifications on how our tap-happy users experience our designs. A design may look fine on a mobile handset, but how does it *feel?* Accounting for touch is of utmost importance as more of the screens in our lives have touch capabilities, but where can you go to learn how to properly execute thoughtful, touch-friendly designs?

You're in luck, because Josh is here to *touch* on these subjects in a big way.

Josh Clark is a treasure trove of touch design insights, and has the uncanny ability to discuss high-level principles and in-the-weeds details alike with clarity and candor. In this book, Josh will help you understand key principles for designing for touch, along with constraints and opportunities for both native platforms and the web. There will be rules of thumb, but also pragmatic advice on when to break those rules

Josh doesn't just bestow years of hard-earned, practical touch design knowledge on you; he delivers it with wit and an enthusiasm for the subject that's downright contagious. I have no doubt by the time you're done with this book, your brain will be bursting with ideas on how to tap, pinch, swipe, and scroll your way to design nirvana. Enjoy!

—**Brad Frost**

FOR DECADES, we explored the digital world with prosthetics called mouse, keyboard, and cursor. We nudged plastic bricks across our desks. We directed onscreen arrows to poke buttons from afar. We clicked icons. We pointed at pixels. But then we started holding those pixels in our hands. Thanks to smartphones, billions of people wrangle touchscreens every day, all day. We now touch information itself: we stretch, crumple, drag, flick it aside. This illusion of direct interaction changes the way we experience the digital world, and it requires designers to adopt new techniques and perspectives. Touch introduces physicality to designs that were once strictly virtual; for the first time, digital designers have to ask themselves, *How does this design feel in the hand?*

That's what this book is about. Touchscreens are everywhere: cabs, vending machines, wristwatches, airplane seats, dressing room mirrors, and of course the gadgets we carry in our pockets and handbags. Nearly half of Americans bought a touchscreen tablet between 2010 and 2014; in 2011, Apple sold more iPads in a single year than all the Macs it sold in the previous twenty-eight years total (http://bkaprt.com/dft/00-01/, http://bkaprt.com/dft/00-02/). And touch has arrived on the desktop, with hybrid tablet/laptop devices that combine keyboard, cursor, and touchscreen.

Despite this inundation of touch devices, most websites remain stubbornly optimized for mouse and cursor. It's past time for designers to catch up with a new generation of web-savvy gadgets. Responsive design jolted the industry with the simple truth that the web is not limited to a single output (the desktop screen). Now comes another revelation: *the web is not limited to a single input.* Touch is one part of an intricate choreography of inputs that might include keyboard, mouse, phone pad, Kinect-style natural gesture, speech, stylus, or dashboard knobs, as well as onboard sensors like camera, audio, GPS, and more. This complex mix affects not only the layout, but also the essential concept of your design. Designing for touch goes way beyond making buttons bigger for fat fingers.

This slender volume gives you a running start with most touch projects, diving into detail on popular form factors—phones, tablets, phablets, and desktop hybrids. I'll describe how design imperatives shift according to software environment, and how designs should flex to make way for non-touch inputs. This means revisiting—and in many cases chucking—the common solutions of the last thirty years of traditional interface design. You'll discover entirely new methods instead, including design patterns, touchscreen metrics, ergonomic guidelines, and interaction metaphors that you can use in your websites and apps right now. The heritage and sources for these techniques may surprise you. We'll search for design patterns in vintage gizmos. We'll plumb video games and car dashboards for interaction lessons. Along the way, you'll learn to surface invisible gestures, discover the subtle power of animation, and find out why a toddler is your best beta tester. Crack your knuckles, limber up those fingers, and let's get started.

A PHYSICAL INTERFACE

THE NEW PHONE WAS A MARVEL, the brainchild of a renowned tech company. It worked in a wholly different way from what came before, yet still charmed novices and technophiles alike. Industry observers called it intuitive, efficient, even fun. The gadget quickly became a status symbol, owned by a select few. As time went on, nearly everyone got one, and we now find its operation so natural that we can barely imagine phones working any other way.

The year was 1963, and the device was Bell Telephone's Touch Tone phone.

A push-button interface replaced the rotary dial, introducing the keypad to millions. As familiar as it seems now, the layout wasn't obvious. To get there, Bell researchers tested sixteen keypad variations, searching for the design that enabled the fastest, most reliable dialing.

"Specifically, we would like to know how push-button design influences user speed, accuracy, and preference in keying telephone numbers," the researchers wrote (http://bkaprt.com/dft/01-01/). "How does performance improve with practice? And are there systematic procedures that users follow in keying

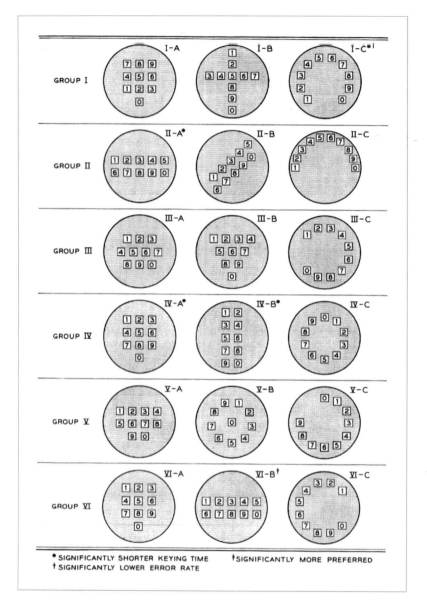

* SIGNIFICANTLY SHORTER KEYING TIME   ‡SIGNIFICANTLY MORE PREFERRED
† SIGNIFICANTLY LOWER ERROR RATE

FIG 1.1: Bell researchers tried sixteen layouts, testing three at a time with six groups, for their new "push-button telephone sets."

numbers?" To find out, they lined up the buttons in a range of shapes—a rainbow, a cross, a diagonal, a circle, even a bulls-eye—before landing on the grid we know today (FIG 1.1). They played with button size, spacing, and typography to reduce mistakes and optimize dialing speed, which they measured to fractions of a second. They asked callers about the keypads' comfort, testing out button tension and whether buttons should click when pressed.

If Bell Telephone's designers were invested in the keypad's visual layout, they were far more concerned with its feel—the context of its physical use. Fast-forward to the current century and our new generation of touch-driven phones and personal devices, and today's digital designers and researchers are learning similar lessons all over again.

TOUCH DESIGN COMBINES DIGITAL AND INDUSTRIAL DESIGN

A phone or tablet presents us with a glass slab (a literal blank slate) and invites us to impose any interface we like. Designing for the screen is nothing new for digital designers, except now these designs have to accommodate *fingers* and thumbs. How do your pixels feel in the hand?

This critical physical dimension calls for us to go beyond strictly visual design and take cues from other design disciplines. When we venture into touch, we verge into industrial design—the craft of shaping physical objects. In the same way real-world objects disappoint when they are physically awkward, your touchscreen interfaces will fail if they are uncomfortable in the hand. This interplay of digits with digital is the crux of designing for touch.

How we hold our gadgets

Where do hands and fingers fall on the device? This question is the linchpin for every form factor this book examines, and the answer tells you how to design your layout for comfort and efficiency. Since we hold phones, phablets, tablets, and laptops very differently, it's no surprise that each of these touchscreen variations has its own UI needs.

Yet these devices also share many consistencies, especially in the crucial role of thumbs. Whether we're tapping away at tiny phones or jumbo tablets, our thumbs do most of the walking. That fact helps us establish sturdy cross-device guidelines. This chapter looks at why the thumb is so important, and reveals fundamental "rules of thumb" based on how we grab screens of all sizes.

The smartphone is of course the device that we hold most. We stare at it for more than 20% of our waking hours, consulting it 221 times per day on average (http://bkaprt.com/dft/01-02/). Let's start with that most familiar of gadgets.

HOLD THE PHONE

In 2013, researcher Steven Hoober took to the streets to observe over 1,300 people tapping away at their phones (http://bkaprt.com/dft/01-03/). He found that in nearly every case, they held their phones in one of three basic grips. At 49%, the one-handed grip was most popular; 36% cradled the phone in one hand and jabbed with the finger or thumb of the other; and the remaining 15% adopted the two-handed BlackBerry-prayer posture, tapping away with both thumbs (**FIG 1.2**).

The study also confirmed what many of us know from our own phone habits: we change grips frequently, depending on convenience and context. We switch between one hand and two, or swap between left and right; sometimes we tap absent-mindedly while doing something else; and other times we stop and give the screen our full attention. Plus: we are nimbly ambidextrous. Hoober found that two-thirds of one-handed grips are in the right hand—a majority, but smaller than the 90% who are right handed. That means many of us favor our non-dominant hand, while using the other to write, drink coffee, hold a baby, or read a book about designing for touch.

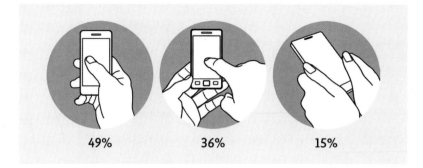

FIG 1.2: Smartphone use is defined by three basic handholds, and we often shift among them.

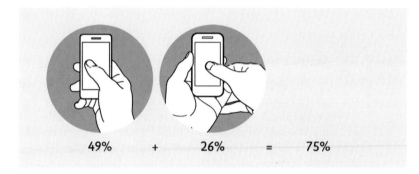

FIG 1.3: Though we often refer to "finger-friendly" designs, the thumb does most of the work.

So while few of us stick with the same grip, we show a distinct preference for one-handed use. And this is where we get to thumbs. When we hold our phones with one hand, the thumb is the only finger comfortably available for tapping. Even when we use both hands, many of us prefer mashing away with our thumb then, too. Of those who cradle their phone in one hand and tap with the other, Hoober discovered that most use their thumb on the screen. Combine all those folks, and it's thumbs up: *thumbs drive 75% of all phone interactions* (FIG 1.3).

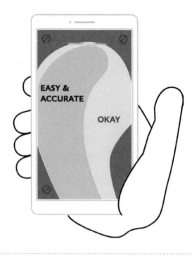

FIG 1.4: The green thumb zone is the most comfortable and accurate region of phone screens for one-handed users. Avoid the red-zone reach, or at least compensate with larger-than-usual touch targets.

EASY & ACCURATE

OKAY

The phone's thumb zone

While a thumb can sweep most of the screen on all but the most oversized phones, only a third of the screen is truly effortless territory: at the bottom, on the side opposite the thumb. For example, if you hold a phone in the right hand, your thumb falls naturally in an arc at the bottom left corner of the screen—no stretching your thumb or shifting the phone required. The same arc shape applies to the two-handed cradle grip, but the arc is larger because the thumb has greater range of motion.

Comfort and accuracy don't perfectly align, however. Within this comfort zone, a separate, fan-shaped arc draws out the most accurate targets for thumb tapping, as uncovered in a study by Qian Fei of Alibaba (http://bkaprt.com/dft/01-04/, subscription required). She also found that, for right-handed users, the bottom and top-right corners were the least accurate thumb zones (**FIG 1.4**).

What about lefties? The thumb zone flips from left to right. But this left-versus-right distinction isn't especially crucial, since most of us switch hands easily (and frequently) depending on context. Even so, optimizing for one hand penalizes the other: the best solutions put core features at screen middle, where left and right thumb zones overlap. In the end, top ver-

최대한을 즐겨라!
삼성 갤럭시 W 출시

FIG 1.5: Samsung's 7″ Galaxy W and similar jumbo devices blur the line between phone and tablet. Photograph courtesy Samsung (http://bkaprt.com/dft/01-06/).

sus bottom is more important than left versus right. No matter which hand you use, screen bottom is most comfortable, while the top demands a stretch. That rule holds true for all phone screens, large or small, but as phones grow to jumbo dimensions, that top-screen stretch becomes a strain.

THE PHABULOUS PHABLET

The first generation of post-iPhone devices consistently featured screens under four inches (as measured across the diagonal), an easy size for one-handed use. By mid-2014, however, a third of mobile web-browsing took place on larger screens as bigger phones shouldered into the marketplace (http://bkaprt. com/dft/01-05/). These super-sized devices fill the spectrum between phone and tablet, a category with the dubious nickname *phablet,* with screens as large as seven inches (**FIG 1.5**). My, how our phones have grown up. And down. And sideways.

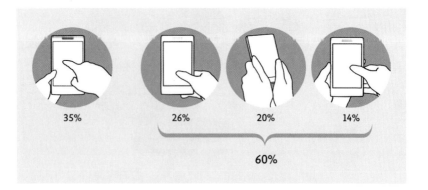

FIG 1.6: Although none of the thumb-driven grips are as common as tapping a phablet with the index finger, they cumulatively account for much more activity.

Despite phablets' gargantuan proportions, people typically handle them like phones, and the three basic grips still apply. Unlike with smaller phones, however, phablet users switch among grips much more often to work the entire screen, and two hands are almost always required. In another study, Hoober and Patti Shank observed that phablet owners use both hands 70% of the time across holds (http://bkaprt.com/dft/01-07/, subscription required). The most popular of these grips, used 35% of the time, is holding a phablet in one hand while tapping with the index finger of the other. But the thumb remains the pointer in charge: *60% of the time, phablet owners tap away with either one thumb or both.*

The phablet's thumb zone

With so much thumb use, the thumb zone is as important for 4"-7" screens as for smaller ones—with a caveat. Phablet folk use two thumbs more often, which creates a pair of mirrored, overlapping thumb zones at the screen's bottom, with a swath of tough-to-reach space at the top. Despite its popularity, the double-thumb zone isn't the one to optimize. Although

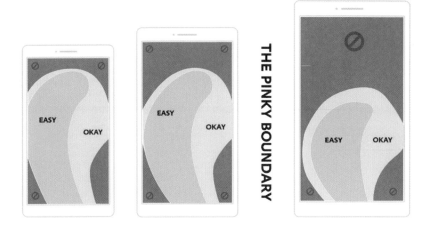

FIG 1.7: The size and shape of the thumb zone shifts when the phone's dimensions require support from the little finger.

we hold phablets with one hand only 25% of the time, the single-thumb grip takes on disproportionate importance for designers, because it has the least range.

This brings us to our first rule of thumb for all form factors: *always accommodate the most constrained grip,* so people can use your interface no matter how they choose to hold their device. On phablets, that means designers should target the single-thumb grip.

Here's a tricky surprise: the one-handed thumb zone is smaller for phablets than for phones. As phone size increases, the thumb zone remains roughly the same shape and position— anchored to screen bottom—until the size hits a tipping point, where the grip shifts to stabilize the phablet. In that handhold, most people slide their pinky finger under the phone to keep it in place, reducing the thumb's range (FIG 1.7).

Even as swaths of the screen become unreachable by thumb alone, some thumb diehards stick with one-handed use, opting to "choke up" on the phone—sliding their hand higher to extend

FIG 1.8: A higher one-handed grip on a phablet nets a bigger thumb zone, but the bottom half of the screen goes out of reach.

their thumb's reach. On phablets, this grip gives people more thumb range overall than the traditional phone grip at screen bottom (**FIG 1.8**). We'll look at the implications of this later in this chapter.

TABLETS: MORE SCREEN MEANS MORE HANDHOLDS

While phones and phablets stay true to three basic grips, there's no such luck with tablets. More screen means more ways to hold, making things unpredictable. The rule of thumb still applies, but with a special headache: the thumb zone isn't consistent even for individual devices; it varies depending on stance and posture.

Standing, we typically use two hands to manage a large tablet like the iPad, holding it halfway up the sides for leverage (hold it too close to the bottom, and the thing keels over). Some wrap an arm around it like a clipboard and tap with the other hand. More likely, though, we're sitting; Hoober and Shank found that 88% of tablet use happens while seated, compared to 19% of phone use. Sitting at a table, we tend to prop up a tablet with one hand at the lower third and, again, tap with the other. Leaning back on the couch, we tend to rest the thing on the belly or nestle it in a blanket, tapping away with one hand.

On top of these shifts in grip, each stance also affects how far away we hold the device: we tend to hold tablets closest while standing, and farthest while reclining. Portrait versus landscape is a mixed bag too, with a 60-40 split in favor of a vertical, or portrait, orientation. As screens get bigger, they also get heavier, and we often lay them down altogether. Hoober and Shank observed that people put large tablets down in nearly two out of three sessions. We rest them flat on a surface (whether table or lap) 40% of the time and upright in a stand 22%. (Smaller 7"-8" tablets are far easier to handle, and 69% of small-tablet use is handheld.) Those surface and stand positions suggest we use large tablets more like traditional monitor screens—or, closer to keyboard-touchscreen hybrids, which we'll get to in a moment—than handheld devices.

The tablet's thumb zone

When we do lift up our tablets, they prove too big to be held and operated with one hand, so two hands come into play. Here again, thumbs play an all-important role. We tend to grab tablets at the sides, and while the specific location wanders up and down, thumbs settle at the middle to top third of the screen. This grip makes the neighboring sides and top corners most friendly to touch (FIG 1.9). On the flip side, the top and bottom edges of tablet screens are hostile zones, because of the necessary reach. The bottom is especially tough, since thumbs are rarely near the bottom—and sometimes that portion of the screen isn't even visible. In the laziest and perhaps most common tablet posture—lying down—the bottom bezel disappears into blankets, sweaters, or soft bellies.

We also, of course, often reach into the middle of the screen; as screen size grows, our hands field ever more surface. However, unlike a mouse cursor, which sweeps effortlessly across a screen's sprawl, our fingers are weighed down by this thing called an arm. This meat pointer goes all the way up to the

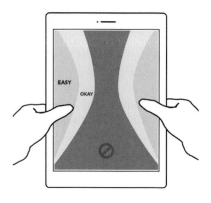

FIG 1.9: Because the tablet grip is typically at the side edges, the thumb zone changes completely from the phone's.

shoulder, and hefting it around the screen demands effort. An interface shouldn't be a physical workout: *group frequent controls within easy reach of thumbs.* Nobody ever broke a sweat twiddling their thumbs.

HYBRIDS AND LAPTOPS: SLAP A KEYBOARD ON IT

If scaling up the screen size has such a dramatic effect on how we hold a device, it should come as no surprise that adding a keyboard shakes things up even more. Our postures, along with our hands and arms, shift yet again to accommodate the keyboard. Until recently, it was rare to spot this hybrid touch-screen-keyboard combination in the wild. And then came Windows 8.

In 2012, Windows introduced touch interaction to the desktop in a total overhaul of the world's most-used operating system. In response, a new category of touch devices—touchscreen laptops and tablet-keyboard combos—flooded the consumer market, creating a new ergonomic environment...and fresh demands on designers.

The wrinkle is that hybrids require us to move our hands between keyboard and touchscreen. Before this generation of hybrids arrived, many dinged the concept as ergonomically untenable: shuttling hands to and fro would be too much effort, resulting in a fatigue dubbed *gorilla arm.* It's a criticism leveled at the science-fiction interfaces of *Minority Report* and *Iron Man* too: *Who wants to work with their arms constantly in the air?* "Touch surfaces don't want to be vertical," a dismissive Steve Jobs said in 2010 (http://bkaprt.com/dft/01-08/). "It gives great demo, but after a short period of time you start to fatigue, and after an extended period of time, your arm wants to fall off."

Research suggests such worries were unnecessary. A study by Intel found that people quickly embrace touch in these new devices, opting for the touchscreen 77% of the time instead of the mouse or keyboard (http://bkaprt.com/dft/01-09/). Despite the availability and precision of the old-school cursor, people said the touchscreen felt more intimate and direct. Other studies have documented this emotional resonance. One reported that people attach more value to products they "touch" on a website versus click with a mouse (http://bkaprt.com/dft/01-10/). When touch is introduced, cold pixels somehow take on the warmth and emotional investment of physical objects. We'll look at this idea more deeply when we poke at gestural interfaces in Chapter 4.

Appeal aside, the touchscreen isn't a complete mouse replacement, but rather a welcome addition to the mix—"like having a laptop with an extra gear," one tester told Intel. With these hybrid devices, people move easily among touch, keyboard, mouse, and trackpad: whatever input seems most convenient. That's a lot of back and forth, though, and you'd think that would only worsen the gorilla-arm problem. Why aren't people's arms going numb? Turns out people quickly figure out how to work the touchscreen without lifting their arms. A study by researcher John Whalen found that when we use touchscreen laptops, we rest our arms alongside the keyboard, keeping a loose grip at the bottom corners of the screen (http://bkaprt.com/dft/01-11/).

The hybrid's thumb zone

This hands-on-the-corners posture defines the thumb zone for hybrids (**FIG 1.10**). Once again, placing touch targets within easy

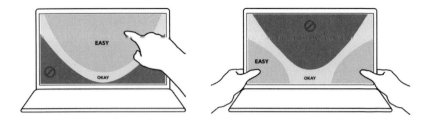

FIG 1.10: The hot zone for thumbs on hybrid devices settles into the bottom corners, nearly opposite the hot zone for the index finger.

reach of the thumbs makes for easy tapping and, in this case, avoids the need to raise the arms.

Not everyone adopts the bottom grip, though. Others (especially newcomers) go free-form, jabbing at the screen with their index finger as they roam the entire interface. For designers, this introduces a head-scratcher; the index finger's hot zone is the reverse of the thumb zone. For index fingers, the center of the screen is easy to hit, and corners are troublesome.

Optimizing for thumbs means a subpar experience for the index finger, and vice versa. One layout has to win, though, and as with every other touch device, studies give the thumb the edge. After a bit of experience with the device, hybrid users soon prefer thumb use for everything, keeping arms planted alongside to thwart gorilla arm (FIG 1.11).

And that's the most striking consistency across the form factors we've reviewed: *thumbs do the driving no matter how large the screen.* The thumb offers the most convenient range of motion with the least possible effort. This physical ease is exactly what Bell Lab's researchers—along with every industrial designer ever—had to take into account as they designed their interfaces. These ergonomic considerations will determine the layouts for your digital interfaces too. We'll start with some general principles for all touch designs, then dive into guidelines for different devices.

FIG 1.11: Expert users of touchscreen hybrids prefer heavy thumb use, even to reach deep into the screen. Photographs by Intel Free Press (http://bkaprt.com/dft/01-12/, http://bkaprt.com/dft/01-13/).

Congratulations! You now have a sturdy understanding of how fingers and thumbs fall on everyday gizmos. Time to turn that knowledge into know-how. The hand position—and, in particular, the thumb zone—tells you the most convenient locations to place controls and content. A few fundamentals hold true across device types.

The rule of thumb

With thumbs the primary pointers, this one's a gimme: consolidate frequent controls into the thumb zones we identified earlier. Perhaps less obvious, it's also crucial to consider what you place *outside* the thumb zone. Put some touch targets—like controls that change data—out of harm's way by making them a little inconvenient. Which actions should be inviting, and which should challenge ever so slightly?

Beyond these matters of convenience and comfort, though, hands pose another physical consideration: you can't see through them.

Hands block the view

So far we've focused on the toil of hands, but the eyes work too; they have to see around your clumsy mitts as you paw at the screen. "You're a better door than a window," my mother told me when I blocked the view. Your design has to contend with the same thing: your hands get in the way. This fact triggers a cascade of design implications.

Content above controls

Glance at any machine from recent centuries, and you'll spot the results of a cardinal principle of industrial design: *content always appears on top*. Whether that content is a calculator display, a meter, or paper in a typewriter, it must appear above hand-operated controls so that fingers don't cover the important stuff (**FIG 1.12**).

FIG 1.12: If the controls of any of these classic contraptions appeared above the "content," your feet, hand, or arm would obstruct your work.

Until now, most digital designers haven't had to deal with this. On the desktop, we've typically done the opposite of "content on top." Desktop software puts menus at the top of the screen or window, and websites usually position navigation at the top of the page. We've gotten away with it, because the tiny cursor has run the show for decades, blocking only a few pixels as it flits across the screen. When you introduce touch, however, fingers and thumbs become the cursor, and they drag hands and arms behind them. It's all too easy to lose the view.

Assume that people will lose sight of everything below an object when they touch it—and of the object itself. This affects how you label controls and confirm touches. In cursor-land, a button can highlight to indicate when it's clicked. With touch, that color change doesn't help anyone when it happens under a fingertip. Present that feedback confirmation above the touch instead. Text labels should likewise sit above controls.

FIG 1.13: Most touchscreen keyboards flash the letter of the selected key above the touch, getting clear of the finger on the screen.

Line of sight combines with ergonomics to dictate the layout of handheld touch interfaces. In particular, these physical constraints drive content to the middle and top of the screen, pushing controls to the sides, corners, and bottom. "Content above controls" is a simple enough rule, but it turns out to be tricky to follow, since the specifics vary according to screen size and platform environment. Operating systems and browsers stake out their own touch-friendly claims to screen space, and designers have to work around their choices. The rest of the chapter explores the caveats and implications for popular platforms and form factors, starting with the small screen.

LAYOUT FOR PHONES

Fingers and thumbs turn desktop conventions on their head; this is literally true when it comes to small-screen layouts. Touchscreen phones flip primary controls like menus and navigation to the bottom of the screen. That puts tap targets in comfortable reach of the thumb, and content comfortably out of the thumb's way. You see this pattern on iPhone, where tab bars and toolbars sink to screen bottom for quick access (**FIG 1.14**).

But consider what's *not* in the thumb zone. iOS convention positions Edit buttons in the upper right, well outside of the thumb zone—available, but only with a stretch. The reason is straightforward: *edit buttons change data.* Tucking them beyond easy reach is an example of defensive design, which helps people avoid mistaps or other actions they might otherwise regret.

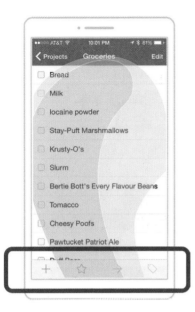

FIG 1.14: In iOS, toolbars anchor the screen bottom in convenient reach of thumbs.

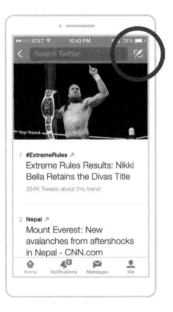

FIG 1.15: Twitter for iPhone banishes the Tweet button way off at top right, reserving the thumb zone for browsing and navigation—and avoiding unintentional tweets. (If only good layout could prevent ill-considered tweets, too, but you're on your own there.)

FIG 1.16: Swarm (left) and Instagram optimize their iPhone app layouts for fast access to the primary task.

Not all data-changing controls have to be exiled from the prime real estate at screen bottom. When an app's main task involves updating that data—and updating it again and again and again—those controls can settle back to the bottom. After all, good design optimizes recurring tasks to make them as ergonomically efficient as possible. The iPhone apps for Swarm and Instagram are useful examples, featuring the core action—checking in or posting a photo—at screen bottom, smack in the middle (**FIG 1.16**). Bonus: that centered position makes the button equally accessible to left and right hands.

So far, so uncomplicated. Then again, we've looked only at iPhone examples. The system-level controls for iOS disappear when you're inside an app, so designers don't have to compete for territory with the platform itself. The same isn't true for other mobile platforms.

FIG 1.17: Don't jam controls against Android's system buttons (or any controls at screen bottom). Instagram (left) and even the stock Android homescreen make this mistake, inviting mistaps in this high-traffic zone.

Make way for the operating system

When the platform elbows in to claim its own screen space, designers have little choice but to move aside, complicating our seemingly simple "content on top" guideline.

Android, for instance, beats app designers to screen bottom with system buttons hugging the baseline of every Android gadget. Android adheres to our rule of thumb, but those buttons are now locked in finger-baffling competition with app controls. If, as app designer, you follow your instinct to put controls below the content, you wind up stacking them atop Android's system buttons (**FIG 1.17**). Cue mistaps.

It's never a good idea to stack controls anywhere on a touch-screen interface; adjacent touch targets tempt wayward fingers and thumbs. Piling controls at the bottom compounds this

FIG 1.18: Facebook places navigation at screen bottom in iOS (left); in Android, the app shifts navigation to the top, steering clear of a traffic jam with Android's system buttons. This in turn pushes the status/photo/check-in controls out of the toolbar and into the News Feed stream.

mistake. For one, the high-traffic thumb zone makes tap errors likely out of sheer volume. For another, the hovering thumb limits screen visibility in that zone; mistakes come faster when you're flying blind.

Alas, the fix is to place controls at the top of the screen, to avoid crowding Android's system buttons (**FIG 1.18**). It's not ideal: you have to stretch to reach the navigation, and when you do, your hand covers the entire screen. But these concessions are better than the bottom-stacking alternative and its inevitable mistaps. In a choice between inconvenience and outright error, inconvenience is the lesser evil.

On small screens running Android, app navigation and controls should float to the top. This is what Android's design guidelines require, reversing the convention for iPhone, whose physical

Home button doesn't create the same kind of competition as Android's system buttons. Android further encourages designers to follow this pattern with the *action bar*, a standard navigation widget that always appears at the top of the screen. So while "content above controls" always applies, it depends on who gets there first. For Android, it's the operating system, and apps have to give way. In iOS, apps have freedom to claim the screen bottom...unless it's a web app.

Make way for the browser

It's an inconvenient fact that websites run inside an emulator we call a web browser. Put another way, *websites are apps inside an app*—a highly variable one at that. While browsers all do the same basic thing, the nuances in how they present web pages are a familiar headache to any web designer. In touch design, the headache pounds when you tally the ways browsers pour their own controls into the screen: buttons on the bottom, buttons on the top, buttons that disappear and reappear depending on how you scroll or where you are on the page.

This browser hodgepodge creates unpredictable UI competition with the websites within. In iPhone's Safari, for example, browser controls live at the bottom edge, and pinning your site navigation there plops your controls atop the browser toolbar—the same problem we saw with Android's system buttons.

Further complicating matters, the screen-bottom toolbar in mobile Safari and other browsers vanishes when you scroll down the page but reappears when you tap the bottom of the screen. If you try to tap a button or link there, you instead summon the toolbar, and your intended tap target skitters up and away, making you chase it with a second tap (**FIG 1.19**).

This brings me to a few sturdy design principles:

Don't pin web navigation to screen bottom. Technical hassles conveniently reinforce this guideline. Web designers are accustomed to freezing onscreen elements in CSS using `position:fixed`. Trying this in mobile browsers, however, is a quick descent into madness, as fixed-positioning support is quirky and uneven in mobile. In some browsers, supposedly fixed elements shake and tremble when you scroll, others roll

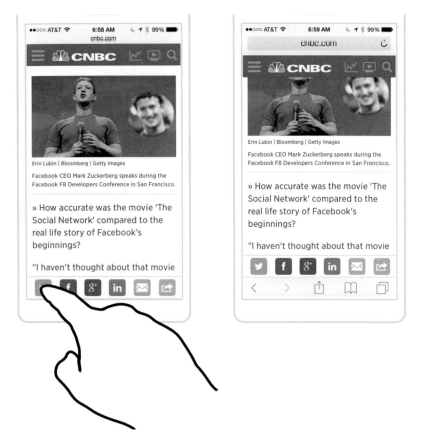

FIG 1.19: In iOS, tapping a link at screen bottom (left) conjures mobile Safari's toolbar instead of activating the link. The page scrolls up to make room, and you have to chase the button up the page with a second tap.

up the page and then snap back, and still others don't respond to position:fixed at all. The resulting stomach acid isn't worth the effort, since pinned navigation on phones is a bad idea to begin with.

Don't pin web navigation to the top, either. Gluing a fixed toolbar *anywhere* on the screen is lousy on phones. Because

FIG 1.20: It's barely a Blahnik! In Barney's old mobile site, that gorgeous high heel in portrait turned into a miserable flat in landscape, squashed in a toolbar sandwich.

the browser's buttons already eat real estate, the last thing you should do is crowd out more content by cramming the top of the page with your own buttons. *But phones are getting bigger and bigger,* the gadget enthusiast argues. *Surely we can spare the room for one measly toolbar?*

While some screens have supersized, others have shrunk. We're awash in tiny-screen smartwatch experiments, and some keyboard-bearing phones still carry postage-stamp screens. You can't assume every screen has the generous dimensions of the most popular smartphones.

Even the biggest smartphones lose their ample height when you flip them into landscape, cutting some websites down to size. Before it was replaced with a responsive redesign, the mobile site for Barney's department store fixed a logo and toolbar at the top. On most phones, this looked fine in portrait. But when you tipped into landscape, the content practically disappeared (**FIG 1.20**). Worse: if you tried to scroll by swiping on top of the logo or toolbar, nothing happened because they were fixed onscreen. You could scroll only by swiping within the sliver of content, a touch target tiny enough to be tough for clumsy thumbs. With so little available screen height, Barney's old design failed.

Putting aside a *fixed* toolbar, the top of the page is hostile for small-screen navigation even when you let it scroll with the rest of the page. When space is limited, don't waste the top of the screen on housekeeping controls; get straight to the content. "Too many mobile web experiences . . . start the conversation off with a list of navigation options instead of content," cautions Luke Wroblewski in *Mobile First* (http://bkaprt.com/dft/01-14/). "Time is often precious on mobile and downloads can cost money, so get people to what they came for as soon as you can."

On the web, lead with content and confine primary navigation to page bottom. That's *page* bottom, not screen bottom. If pinning controls to a fixed location on the page is poor form, the solution is to put them inside the page itself. To do so, Wroblewski champions a useful design pattern, which you can see at work at The Session website (http://bkaprt.com/dft/01-15/): the navigation *appears* to be tucked behind a button at the top of the screen (**FIG 1.21**).

The menu's quick reveal feels like an overlay, but in reality, it's an anchor link that jumps you to the navigation section at page bottom. Tap the arrow button or the browser's back button to return to the top of the page. The essential markup couldn't be simpler:

```
<a href="#navigation">Menu</a>

. . .

<ul id="navigation">
  <li><a href="/one">Item one</a></li>
  <li><a href="/two">Item two</a></li>
  <li><a href="/three">Item three</a></li>
</ul>
```

FIG 1.21: Tap the arrow-shaped menu button at the top (left), and the screen fills with navigation options. In fact, the button takes you to the navigation's home at the bottom of the page.

This approach has several advantages, Wroblewski writes:

This design uses a minimum amount of navigation elements (just a single link at the top), gives people an opportunity to pivot and explore when they get to the end of content, doesn't duplicate the content of another menu, and (best of all) only requires a simple anchor link to work. That's right: no fancy JavaScript, overlays, or separate navigation pages to maintain—just an anchor that links to the bottom of the page. That's like HTML 0.

HTML 0?!? But that's like *five* HTMLs away from what I want! We all swoon from time to time for a bit of JavaScript-spiked interactive sugar. While I prefer the elegant simplicity of anchor-link navigation, where options conveniently appear as you finish the page's content, others may find it too simple. If so, consider keeping the anchor-link markup, and use progressive enhancement to upgrade the menu to a more interactive experience. By providing JavaScript and CSS for supporting browsers, you can convert that navigation to an overlay that dissolves into place, or a panel that slides in from the side. For less capable browsers (or should the JavaScript fail to load), the navigation falls back to the anchor-link nav in the footer.

All together now

The simple "content above controls" rule gets complicated when the operating system or browser claims a phone's premium real estate. In the end, though, it boils down like this:

- On iPhone, put app controls at screen bottom.
- On Android, put app controls at screen top.
- For the web, favor navigation at page bottom (not screen bottom).

Just as software platforms shift layout guidelines, so does hardware. We know handholds adapt to fit the shape, size, and weight of the gadget. So what happens to your interface layout when the touchscreen embiggens?

LAYOUT FOR PHABLETS

As screen size heads north of five inches, your layout has to accommodate the screen outside the thumb's reach. Despite phablet users' readiness to shift their grips to get at content, it's our job to limit that extra effort as much as possible. Herding frequent taps into the one-handed thumb zone (the most constrained grip) is the best way to do this. Sharp readers—yes, you!—remember that even the one-handed thumb zone moves up and down the device as screen size increases. Though you can't simply scale up your phone layout for phablets, some basics still apply.

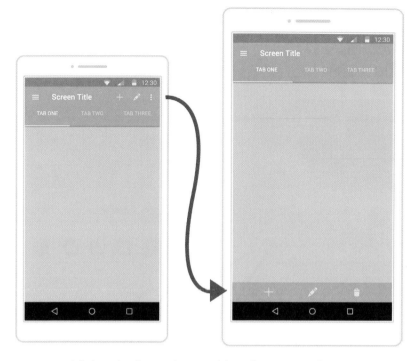

FIG 1.22: By default, Android's action bar consolidates all navigation and options at the top of the screen (left). The split action bar (right) moves action icons to screen bottom, providing easy thumb access on phablets.

For phablet apps, place navigation and frequent controls at screen bottom. No matter the handhold, the top of a phablet screen is always a difficult reach. As with smaller phones, follow "content above controls" to keep frequent tap targets within reach *and* out of the way of content. The exception is Android. Instead of piling all controls at the top as you would for smaller screens, opt to slide some frequent controls down to a separate toolbar at screen bottom (**FIG 1.22**). This is the split action bar design pattern, which was originally developed for tiny screens but is now proving useful for jumbo gadgets.

This still isn't great. Stacking controls on phablets invites the same mistaps as it does on smaller phones. Since it's nearly

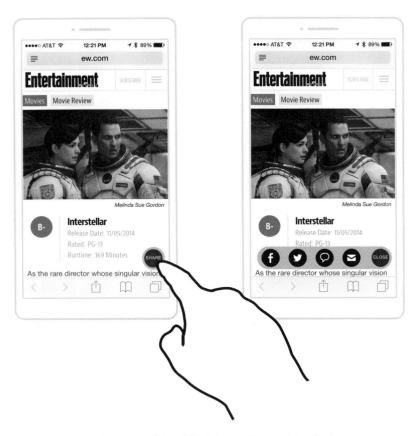

FIG 1.23: On *Entertainment Weekly's* mobile site (http://m.ew.com), a floating trigger button (left) expands to show sharing options (right).

impossible to reach top screen controls one-handed, however, moving the controls into range is worth the risk. At least thumb tappers can reach the buttons in the first place. As noted earlier, platform pressures constantly force designers to compromise. When in doubt, the lesser evil is always the option that at minimum allows basic access.

A *floating trigger button* is a useful workaround. These buttons nest in the screen's bottom corner, hovering in place as the rest of the page scrolls past. You can use a trigger button

FIG 1.24: A floating trigger button, like the action button at bottom right, lets you include one or more primary actions at screen bottom without conflicting with Android's system buttons.

for a screen's primary action—"add a photo," "check in," "new message"—or morph it into a mini toolbar or radial menu of related actions. (You'll learn more about radial menus in Chapter 4.) When I led the design of *Entertainment Weekly*'s responsive mobile website, we used a floating trigger button to offer quick access to sharing tools across screen sizes (FIG 1.23). Tap the button to reveal a toolbar of options.

Wait, shouldn't we avoid stacking controls at screen bottom? Yep, this is another compromise to bring phablet controls within reach. The good news: a small, expanding button lessens the stacking penalty of a full-width toolbar. In Android's UI lingo, a trigger button is called a *floating action button* (FIG 1.24); check out Android's design guidelines for more on button-spacing (http://bkaprt.com/dft/01-16/).

Alternatively, show visual controls at screen top, with fallback interaction below. A second thumb-friendly option for phablets is to keep tab controls at the top but supplement them with swipe navigation in the main canvas below (FIG 1.25). This

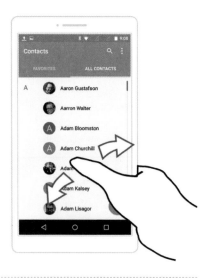

FIG 1.25: Contacts in Android offers swipeable tabs. Reach up to tap the Favorites or All Contacts tab, or swipe anywhere on the screen to move between the two. (Tabs are a standard component in the Android operating system, and swipeability is baked in for easy use by developers.)

pattern works well for navigating content that is organized into tabbed views. People can reach for the tabs to switch views, but for jumbo screens, it's more convenient to swipe the content directly. The popular pull-to-refresh gesture offers similar benefits, allowing you to tug down from anywhere on the screen without reaching for a button.

For web navigation, stick with the anchor-link menu pattern. The technical limitations and competition with browser controls at play on small screens apply to phablets too. The best fix is a menu link at the top that jumps you down to navigation at the bottom. Admittedly, the menu link's top-corner position is well outside the thumb zone, but that matters less than you'd think. I see this all the time in user research: people turn to main navigation as a last resort, when they can't find what they want in the body of the page. Which means placing navigation at page bottom delivers it when it's most needed (without any thumb stretching).

Avoid the cross-phablet stretch. Most mere mortals don't have thumbs that can reach clear to the other side of a phablet: the left side of the screen is outside the right thumb's striking range in one-handed use. Avoid tap targets that hug the left

FIG 1.26: Samsung's one-handed mode (left) shrinks phablet UIs down to manageable phone size, while Apple's Reachability feature (right) slides the top of the screen down within reach. Left photograph by Kārlis Dambrāns (http://bkaprt.com/dft/01-17/); right photograph courtesy Apple (http://bkaprt.com/dft/01-18/).

or right edge too tightly. In the main body of the page, favor targets that stretch at least a third into the screen—or even better, full width.

But don't scale up gesture sizes along with screen size. Say that an interface lets you swipe across a menu to reveal actions. Use the same swipe distance you would for a phone—don't make people span the entire phablet to trigger a feature. Just because you wield a giant phone doesn't mean you have giant hands; size gestures to the hand, not the screen.

Move mountains. Most interfaces are fixed landscapes that we sweep across. We move to the buttons; they never come to us. But it doesn't have to be that way. Samsung created a special One-handed Operation mode for its jumbo Android phones (**FIG 1.26**). When you turn on the feature, the interface shrinks to a regular phone size, everything within range for one-handed thumb tapping. In effect, you temporarily turn your big phone into a small one. Unfortunately, that huge gorgeous screen goes unused, undoing the reason for having a phablet.

Apple took a different approach in iOS with a feature it calls "reachability" (**FIG 1.26**). Touch the Home button twice, and the interface slides down so that the top half of an app moves to the bottom half of the screen, bringing it within thumb range, and springing back when you're done. This makes top controls as

FIG 1.27: *Time* (http://time.com) offers a side tab that slides open a drawer full of recent news items when you tap it.

easy to hit as if you had shifted your grip higher on the phone, without the effort. Another advantage: unlike Samsung's take, this sliding approach doesn't alter the size or layout of the touch targets.

While these solutions from Apple and Samsung are at the operating-system level, websites can put sliding panels to use too. Instead of sliding the interface up or down, though, a more practical tack in web pages is sliding a menu drawer in from the edges. A small button or tab in the thumb zone conjures the menu, its options convenient for one-handed use (**FIG 1.27**).

A caveat: the side edges are outside the comfortable thumb zone for phablets, though still much easier to reach than the top. (You can sidestep this cross-device reach by also letting

FIG 1.28: iPad apps Instapaper (left) and Twitter both show good alternative placements of controls in the tablet thumb zone.

people swipe the screen to slide the drawer open in a fallback interaction.) In general, side controls make more sense for two-handed use, which is why they're most successful on larger tablets. That's our cue to bump up to the phablet's big sibling.

LAYOUT FOR TABLETS

Layouts for large tablets depart sharply from smaller screens. While phones and phablets prefer screen bottom for frequent touch targets, tablet thumb zones move up and out, favoring the sides and top corners (**FIG 1.28**). As the top of the screen becomes more important for touch, this aligns with the visual experience too. The bigger the screen, the harder it is to take in the whole thing at a glance, as we can on a phone, and so our eyes—like our thumbs—naturally land on the top half of tablets. The design's information hierarchy should reflect that.

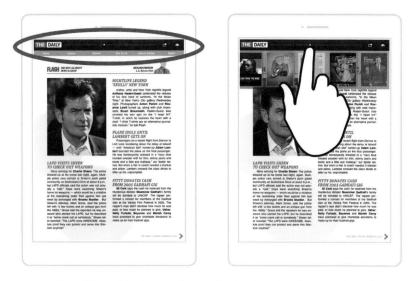

FIG 1.29: *The Daily*'s scrubber bar reveals page thumbnails, only to have your finger block them from view. As with most touch interfaces, the center top of the screen is a poor place for controls.

While the top corners are great for frequent touch targets, the top middle is outright hostile. Reach aside, the top middle demands that you cover the screen and all its content. The now-defunct iPad magazine *The Daily* offered a sliding scrubber bar at top center to scan through the issue's pages (**FIG 1.29**), but when you used it, the hand covered the thumbnails. You had to resort to weird contortions to even see the issue covers while working the slider.

The Daily's misstep kicks up an exception to the top-corner guideline for tablet controls. In some cases, controls should go to the bottom edge, even though the bottom is the most unfriendly region of tablets for both touch and visuals. This exception is necessary when you need to see the effects of those controls in the main canvas. *When controls browse or change content, place them below or to the side of that content, never above.*

The *Sydney Morning Herald*'s iPad app, for example, has a novel way to scan all articles in the day's issue by dragging

FIG 1.30: The *Sydney Morning Herald*'s iPad app lists the page's headlines when you tap the page-indicator dots at screen bottom. The control's position leaves the headlines unobscured.

your finger along an index of page indicators at screen bottom (**FIG 1.30**). That control reveals a tall list of headlines, so it's an acceptable compromise to place those controls at screen bottom; if the controls were at the top, your hand would cover the list when you touched them.

So do tablet controls take top or bottom? Split it like so:

- Top corners are ideal for navigation and one-tap tools for actions like sharing, favoriting, or deleting.
- The bottom edge is *acceptable* for controls that browse or preview content in the canvas above. (If room allows, however, the better bet is to place these tools at the edges, which also keeps hands and fingers out of the way.)

The bottom edge becomes far more friendly when your touch-screen stands upright and sprouts a keyboard. The hybrid/ laptop thumb zone favors the bottom edge and corners, and your layout should too. *Cluster primary controls and gestures at bottom corners and sides.* This ain't the way we usually do it, right? Most widescreen designs traditionally pin primary controls like navigation and toolbars at the top or middle of the screen, an area well outside the crucial thumb zone. Touch forces us to reevaluate. The best touch-optimized Windows apps, for example, shift frequent controls from screen center to *edge regions:* swipe from the right edge to pull out the Windows action bar, and swipe up from the bottom to surface the task bar (**FIG 1.31**).

When they don't organize primary controls in these offscreen drawers, well-behaved Windows apps align those controls along the left or right side, or across the bottom. Face-book for Windows arrays main navigation along the left edge and the chat sidebar along the right. The Xbox music app places its player controls on the bottom. In each case, primary controls are within easy reach of corner-dwelling thumbs (**FIG 1.32**).

Bottom-heavy works fine for native apps, but it's more complicated for the web. Browsers are clueless at detecting what kind of input device they're dealing with. There's no reliable way to find out if a device has a touchscreen, a keyboard, a mouse, or some combination of all three. In other words, *the browser has no idea if it's running on a tablet, hybrid, or laptop.* Native software gets much more information about the device at hand, so native app designers can do much more to tailor the touch experience to the device.

We need new web-design techniques to hedge for all types of large-screen displays. There's nowhere to go but up: most widescreen web layouts are not yet optimized for touch on *any* of these devices. That's because many of us still operate under the assumption that widescreen means desktop, and that desktop means mouse and keyboard. Both assumptions were leaky to begin with, but with tablets and hybrids they've stopped holding water altogether. As a result, widescreen web-

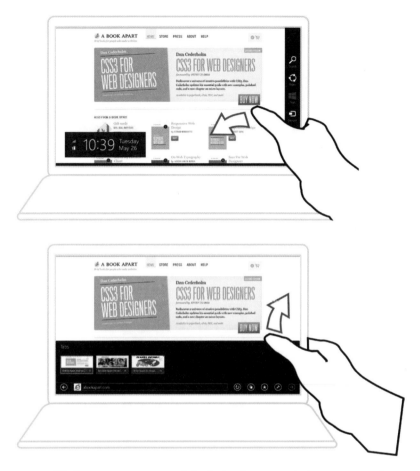

FIG 1.31: Windows system gestures optimize for hands at rest at the bottom corners. In Windows 8, swipe from the right edge (top) to summon the Charms bar—replaced by the Action bar in Windows 10—or swipe up from the bottom to summon the task bar.

sites challenge our clumsy fingers and thumbs with small touch targets for links and <select> menus, or they lean on hover interactions that can't be triggered by touch at all.

We need to change the way we *think* about designing for larger screens. We need to change our thinking about screens, period. They deceive and distract us. What we think we know

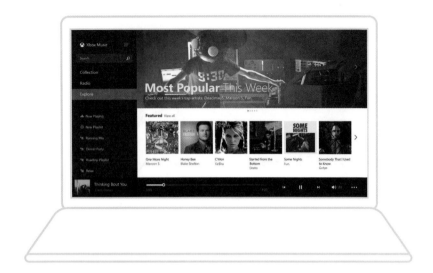

FIG 1.32: Edge controls put frequent tap targets in easy reach of resting thumbs. The Xbox Music app (top) snaps navigation to the left edge and player controls along the bottom. Facebook (bottom) lets you browse categories with your left thumb and the chat sidebar with your right.

about screens often takes our designs in the wrong direction. Turns out that pixels don't work the way most of us think they do, screen size has nothing to do with touch, and browsers don't even know what gadgets are connected to them. This makes it tricky to adapt reliably to the physical demands that have been the focus of this chapter. The trouble for touchscreen designers is less in those mechanics than in the mechanism— the screen itself.

THE UNRELIABLE SCREEN

THE SCREEN HAS LONG SEEMED a trusty canvas as the base for our visual interfaces. For most of web design's short history, screens were reassuringly stable. They kept the same aspect ratio for decades, and though they gradually grew in size, they did so at a steady pace. The web design industry settled on standard widths—beginning with 600 pixels in the 1990s, then 800 pixels around 2000, then 980, and finally 1200. And then, suddenly, this fixed-width illusion exploded with the mobile revolution and its bevy of screen shapes and sizes.

Responsive design is the new normal, and thanks to CSS media queries, we've adapted our designs to pocket-sized containers. But touchscreens and other emerging input devices pose stubborn new challenges, like wide-ranging pixel densities and mercurial touch support, that media queries aren't (yet) equipped to handle. Screens no longer provide the solid design footing they once appeared to.

Our mission is to build solid physical interactions on top of this squishy virtual foundation. This chapter explains how to bring some order to the unreliable screen. We'll uncover cross-device interactions that work with or without a touch-screen. We'll explore the pinch-and-zoom world of dynamic viewports and suss out how to size touch targets even when you don't know the screen's pixel density. Most important, we'll look at what you can and can't know about screens—and what you can safely assume: very little.

Even the simple question, *does this device have a touchscreen?* resists a straight answer. Browsers offer no way to know for certain. Ideally, we'd be able to tweak our CSS to accommodate multiple input types in the same way responsive design accounts for multiple output types (e.g., screen sizes). Unfortunately, we don't yet have surefire tools for detecting a device's inputs. Keyboard, touch, mouse, voice, or Kinect-style natural gesture—we can't peg how the user pilots the browser.

SCREEN SIZE IS A LOUSY WAY TO DETECT TOUCH

Without better tools, we've relied on the dubious assumption that screen size tells us something about the input. "If it's a small screen, it's touch. If it's a big screen, it's mouse-driven." That distinction was already in trouble with large tablets like iPad, and hybrids shatter it with touch on full-sized screens. At the fringes, enormous picture-window tablets are also emerging, with screen sizes headed north of 20 inches. Yet designers still talk about "mobile" and "desktop" layouts (touch versus mouse) when they really mean narrow and wide screens. It's past time to stop conflating screen size with input type, but how?

Though media queries don't yet target touch devices, that will change with CSS4. The new pointer media query targets gadgets with *fine* or *coarse* pointing tools—or even no pointer at all, like voice- or keyboard-only interfaces (http://bkaprt.com/dft/02-01/). A mouse, trackpad, stylus, or any other precision gizmo counts as fine, while fingers are coarse. This lets us create specific rules that are kinder to fingers and thumbs. For example, to make input fields taller, you'd use `pointer` like so:

```
/* Make input fields taller for touch */
@media (pointer:coarse) {
  input[type="text"] {
    min-height:44px;
  }
}
```

Although `pointer` is a definite improvement, its either/or approach to coarse versus fine oversimplifies our input environment. As hybrids have already shown us, the same device can have more than one input. When you have a mix of coarse and fine pointers, the `pointer` media query relies on what the browser considers to be the "primary" input. A tablet with a third-party keyboard would likely consider its touchscreen as primary—`pointer` would return coarse—but a touchscreen laptop might consider its trackpad the main input, and `pointer` would return fine.

`pointer` would be vastly more useful if we could target specific combinations. As we learned in Chapter 1, the layout for a touch-keyboard hybrid should differ from that of a touch-only tablet, because the ergonomics differ. That makes it important to identify both the availability of touch and whether it's combined with other input types. While we're at it, it'd be great to have HTTP headers that announce to the backend server what type of device it's dealing with:

"Hi, I'm a touchscreen!"
"Howdy, I'm a touch-keyboard hybrid."
"Greetings, I have no screen at all..."

But that's all slated for the future. Until we get these *"Hello, my name is"* name tags in CSS or HTTP, we have to make do. We can come frustratingly close to detecting a touchscreen by using JavaScript to sniff for touch events and adding a "touch" class to the DOM's `document` element. For a quick but somewhat naive test, you can check for the presence of ontouchstart or MaxTouchPoints (msMaxTouchPoints in Internet Explorer):

```
<script>
// if the browser supports touch, add class 'touch'
    to body element
if ( 'ontouchstart' in window ||
      window.navigator.MaxTouchPoints ||
      window.navigator.msMaxTouchPoints )
{
    document.getElementsByTagName('body')[0].className
    += ' touch';
}
</script>
```

And from there, add this to your CSS to boost the size of touch targets:

```
/* Make input fields taller for touch */
.touch input[type="text"] {
    min-height:44px;
}
```

This isn't perfect. First, this approach tests the browser to see if *the software* supports touch, but overlooks the hardware. Just because a browser understands touch doesn't mean that the device does. Touch-supporting browsers on gadgets without touchscreens sometimes report that touch events are available, which results in false positives. You're asking the *software* if it supports touch, after all, and some browsers will truthfully say they do, even when they're running on hardware that doesn't. Second, not all touch browsers make touch events available in JavaScript, which gives you false negatives (this will bite you in Opera Mini and older Symbian and Windows Phone 7 devices).

The gloomy upshot: we can't reliably know if we're dealing with a touchscreen, at least for now. Our only real option is to guess. And we have only one good guess to make.

Because any device *might* be used for touch, we must assume it will be. In the face of this uncertainty, it's our job to ensure that the layout is accessible to both cursors and fingers. Every web design—and the same goes for native desktop apps—should be finger friendly. That's not how we do it now. Our "settled" design strategies don't address touch and cursor. A new desktop design language is needed, one that replaces cursor-only interactions with conventions flexible enough to handle several potential input styles. It may ultimately prove impossible to support *every* input type—or combination of input types—with a single interface. Perhaps we'll need to offer different modes that people can switch among according to their wont. (The video site Vimeo, for example, lets users click a "couch mode" button to change the interface to something more appropriate for big-screen TV viewing.) The last thing we should do, though, is punt. The ideal of the web, after all, is to be a platform that can be accessed from any device, no matter what its input or output method. For now, that means opening up all desktop layouts for easy finger-tapping, and that at least is a surmountable challenge.

DESIGNING FOR BOTH TOUCH AND CURSOR

While screen size is a poor way to detect touch, size and form still shape touch interactions—which is why phones, tablets, and hybrids each have different thumb zones. Once we assume all screens are touchscreens, screen size can inform which thumb-friendly layout to shoot for. Targeting phones and phablets is easy enough, since the thumb zone stays consistent for all screens of those sizes. Things get dicey, however, for tablets and hybrids; since their screen sizes overlap, size-based media queries can't help us trigger tablet- and hybrid-specific layouts.

FIG 2.1: When you overlay the tablet's thumb zone (left, yellow) with the hybrid's thumb zone (middle, blue), they intersect in an area that hugs the left and right corners: effectively, the bottom half of the tablet's thumb zone.

Instead, we have to make calls (and compromises) to create layouts that favor thumbs in both devices, along with interactions that work for hands and cursors.

Target the common thumb zone: left and right edges

The thumb zones for tablets and desktop hybrids differ, but they do overlap. This common thumb zone converges at the screen's left and right sides, establishing a touch-friendly area for both form factors (**FIG 2.1**). Place frequent touch targets here.

In particular, favor the left edge for primary controls. Steven Hoober and Patti Shank found that 84% of index-finger users point with their right hand (http://bkaprt.com/dft/01-07/). In most cases, that leaves the left hand anchoring the screen, for easy thumb navigation at the left edge. As for "primary controls," don't rush to assume those should be a site's main navigation. Remember, for most people, the traditional main-menu nav is a last resort—used only when they can't find what they want in the body content. Clear nav menus are still important in telling people what a site is about, but they don't rate prime interaction real estate. Instead, primary controls are *the things people actually use on your site.* For a media company, those might be sharing links (**FIG 2.2**). For a commerce site, they're probably "Add to cart" and "Checkout." Whatever buttons people mash most, plunk those into the left-edge thumb zones.

FIG 2.2: UserTesting (http://bkaprt.com/dft/02-02/) adds sharing buttons to the left gutter of article pages at wide widths (e.g., tablet and desktop form factors). Easy thumb tapping makes for easy sharing.

Reduce the number of taps

Physical interfaces take physical work to operate. The larger the touchscreen, the more effort and precision it requires. Save people time and elbow grease by reducing the number of taps and interactions needed to move through your design. Select menus, text entry, carousels, and other web widgets swing from easy convenience with keyboard and mouse to dreary burdens on touchscreens. (Chapter 3 digs into the alternatives for faster interactions.)

Hover is an enhancement

Grab an iPad and float your finger above the screen to see what happens. Nothing? Hover can be useful in cursor-driven contexts, but it leaves you hanging on most touchscreens. (Certain stylus interfaces are an exception: Samsung's S Pen stylus

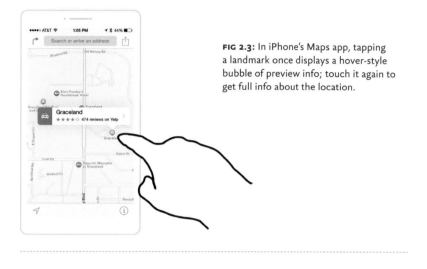

FIG 2.3: In iPhone's Maps app, tapping a landmark once displays a hover-style bubble of preview info; touch it again to get full info about the location.

triggers hover events when you hold it just above the glass.) As hover isn't universally available, including on speech- and text-only browsers, treat it as an enhancement. It's okay to use hover for shortcuts and quick peeks at content for browsers and devices that support it, but don't make hover the only route to get there.

A tap can still be effective at providing hover-like glimpses of information. Map interfaces routinely let you tap a location once to glean summary info and then a second time to jump into full detail (**FIG 2.3**). This little two-step is how most touch web browsers handle mouseover events and CSS :hover states, triggering mouseover/hover on the first touch and a proper click on the second.

The forthcoming standard for CSS4 media queries will introduce a new hover media query that controls styles based on the device's hover ability (http://bkaprt.com/dft/02-03/). This lets you hide and reveal content on hover-capable gadgets, for example, but keep content visible for those that are not (like an iPad with touchscreen-only input):

```
@media (hover) {
  /* CSS for devices that hover; hide and
     show on hover */
  .metadata { display: none }
  .metadata:hover { display: block }
}
@media (hover: none) {
  /* CSS for devices that do not hover;
     always visible */
  .metadata { display: block }
}
```

The story gets more complicated for devices with multiple inputs. Say that you have a touchscreen tablet with an optional mouse. In that case, hover works like the pointer media query discussed earlier: it falls in line with whatever the browser decides is the device's primary input. As touch is our example tablet's primary input (the mouse is an optional add-on), the browser would identify itself as a non-hovering gizmo—*even when the mouse is used.* If you wanted to create rules that would match if any input (primary or not) offers hover, you would use the new any-hover media query:

```
@media (any-hover: hover) {
  /* at least one of the attached inputs
     DOES have hover */
}
```

There's likewise a rule to match browsers where none of the inputs have hover:

```
@media (any-hover: none) {
  /* at least one of the attached inputs
     DOES NOT have hover */
}
```

When to use hover versus any-hover? The distinction here is convenience. hover is triggered when the gadget's main input interface makes it effortless to hover. any-hover, by contrast, gets triggered anytime hover is at all possible, even if it requires a secondary input device or extra effort (some browsers trigger hover events with a long press, for example). Things can get even more tangled: while the browser in our example gadget would follow the CSS rules for the hover:none media query, it would also still honor the :hover pseudo-class when you use that optional mouse to hover over an element. So, while it might seem surprising, this CSS rule would indeed be triggered:

```
@media (hover: none) {
  /* the device's primary input does not
     have hover */

  a:hover {
    /* but a secondary input might be able to
       hover, so anticipate that use */
    color: red;
  }
}
```

Here, the browser follows the designer's wishes for the best possible layout for the primary input (touch), while respecting the secondary input (mouse). Welcome to the wild, woolly world of designing for multi-input devices.

Go big or go home

Your screen size might change, but your fingers don't. From tiny phone to jumbo desktop, touch targets must be large enough to welcome the human hand. An overwhelming 83% of websites, per a 2013 Google study, hamper users with too-small targets (http://bkaprt.com/dft/02-04/). We need to make tap targets too big to fail, so people can tap without crossing their eyes in concentration or jabbing at the screen with miss after miss. Small <select> menus, tiny text in utility menus, and itty-bitty footer links all have to bump up in size to be usable.

How big is big enough? The answer starts with a more fundamental question: *What's the size of a fingertip?* The human finger ranges from 8 mm wide for a child to 18 mm for the

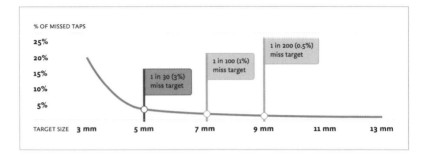

FIG 2.4: Microsoft's touchscreen accuracy study found that 7 mm is the minimum touch target size, with diminishing returns beyond 9 mm.

Incredible Hulk, a daunting disparity. Happily, finger width is far less relevant than the size of the fingertip as a contact point on the screen. No matter how chunky or dainty a person's fingers may be, the surface area of fingertips against the screen is remarkably consistent.

THE GOOD-ENOUGH SIZE: 7 MM

A touch target of 7 mm, or about ¼″, delivers the bulls-eye across devices. In a study of phone and desktop touchscreens, Microsoft researchers tested people's ability to touch varied target sizes (http://bkaprt.com/dft/02-05/). No surprise: the smaller the button, the more mistaps. At 5 mm, people missed the target one out of thirty times—unacceptably high. At 7 mm, the number dropped to one out of a hundred—not bad—and at 9 mm, the error rate dropped to one out of 200. Buttons beyond 9 mm brought only tiny improvements (**FIG 2.4**).

For most screens, 7 mm yields a good-enough result for workaday touch targets. For critical, can't-miss situations where errors might cause severe regret (the "Release the Kraken!" button), pumping the size up to 9 mm or even 11 mm makes sense. You might also do so for close, delete, or other destructive actions where touching the wrong target requires "more than two gestures, five seconds, or a major context change to

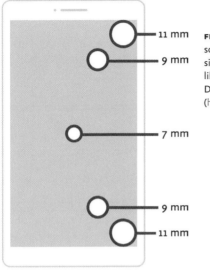

FIG 2.5: While 7 mm is a sturdy size for screen center, it's helpful to boost the size to 9 mm or 11 mm in stretch locations like the corners or top/bottom edges. Data from Steven Hoober and Patti Shank (http://bkaprt.com/dft/01-07/).

correct," as noted in Microsoft's interface guidelines (http://bkaprt.com/dft/02-06/). On spacious tablet and desktop screens, it's fine to bump all touch targets to 9 mm—a size that buys you extra security without much cost in those cases. Even there, the smaller size delivers accurate results. **For most touch targets, consider 7 mm your absolute minimum.**

LOCATION, LOCATION, LOCATION: LAYOUT AND TARGET SIZE

Not all tap targets are equal. For phones, the fan-shaped thumb zone is much more accurate than other parts of the screen. Translation: *touch targets should be larger the farther they are from the thumb zone.* In particular, super-size the four corners to 11 mm or even larger to improve accuracy (**FIG 2.5**).

As always, specific audience needs trump all. If you're designing for people with poor motor control—the very young or very old, for example—then even larger touch targets may be in order, at 10-15 mm.

Great! But...millimeters? Millimeters aren't exactly go-to units when we're spinning CSS or writing mobile apps. What do these numbers mean in more familiar units? Etch this number in your noggin: 44.

MAKE TAP TARGETS A MINIMUM OF 44 (PIXELS, POINTS, OR DP)

Forty-four is your magic number, the size that delivers 7 mm touch targets across platforms. Use 44 *pixels* on the web. For native apps, use platform-specific units: iOS takes *points,* while Android has *density-independent pixels,* or *dp.* This trio of units differs only in name; the point and dp are sized at 160 dpi, just like the typical web pixel. So you can use the same numbers, no matter the platform. At 160 dpi, 44 pixels is .275", or 7 mm—voilà!

(But wait, not all screens are 160 dpi, right? Since pixel density varies wildly from device to device, don't web pixels themselves vary in size too? Short answer: no. Longer answer: see the end of this chapter. In the meantime, put your trust in 44.)

While 44 is your base minimum, it's okay to go bigger—particularly for larger screens—to offer easy, take-no-risks tap targets. When we apply our 160 dpi math, 9 mm translates to 57 pixels. If you really want to go big, 10mm is 63 pixels and 11 mm works out to 69 pixels.

On the other hand, sometimes you're forced to go smaller. Ideally, all touch targets would be at least 7 mm square, 44 × 44, but small screens often demand compromise. The iPhone's keyboard, for instance, has keys that are 44 tall but 30 wide—similarly, in landscape view, the buttons are 44 wide but 38 tall, to fit the full QWERTY keyboard onscreen.

When limited space puts the squeeze on tap targets, here's what I've found works best: as long as a target is at least 44 pixels in one dimension, you can, if you must, squeeze the other as small as 30 pixels, a tad more than 4.75 mm. That means: *the practical minimum size for any tap target is 44 x 30 (or 30 x 44).*

But pixel units aren't exactly welcome in these parts. In responsive design, it's considered best practice to use *ems* for size and layout (http://bkaprt.com/dft/02-03/). Ems are relative units keyed to text size; an em matches the height of the current font. Relative units might seem at odds with fixing a minimum physical size to our touch targets, but we're in luck. Nearly all browsers default to the same font size, 16 pixels, which translates to the magic minimum of 2.75 ems:

```
2.75em = 44px = 7mm
3.5625em = 57px = 9mm
```

Ems quickly get messy, though, because they're relative to the font size of the parent element. So if you size a button to 2.75em inside a block of 12px text, the button will be 33px, not 44px. Our careful math is undone.

Cue the heroic music, as *rem* swoops in to the rescue. Rem stands for "root em," or the font size of the root element—the <html> element in the DOM. No matter how font sizes might change throughout the document, that fundamental rem size is constant because it always refers to the size of that single root element. Most browsers set root font-size to 16px, so 2.75rem equals 44px.

Rems were introduced in CSS3, so older browsers won't understand them (looking at you, IE8). To aid those browsers, specify size in pixels first and define it again in rems:

```
html { font-size: 16px; } /* set default font size
   to standard 16 pixels */
.touch { height: 44px; height: 2.75rem } /* 7 mm */
.touch-big { height: 57px; height: 3.5625rem }
   /* 9 mm */
```

FIG 2.6: Skype's dial-pad design jams the buttons next to each other but avoids mistaps by making the buttons much larger than 44 pixels.

Just like that, we have a consistent rule for touch targets in every browser, using a relative unit that will scale and flex with all the responsive mojo you care to muster.

DON'T CROWD ME

Touch-target spacing is as important in preventing errors as sizing. The closer targets are, the larger they should be. Likewise, the smaller they are, the more you should space them out.

Microsoft's design guidelines offer a stalwart standard: space 7 mm touch targets by at least 2 mm (13 pixels or 0.8125 rems). If you want your targets flush against one another, make them a minimum of 9 mm (57 pixels or 3.5625 rems).

Whew. So we've talked sizing, spacing, and sticking with rems. Let's back up and get physical—with pixels. When we're dealing with relative units and screens with varying pixel densities, how can a single "44" guarantee a specific physical size? Strap in, friend—the ride is about to get a little bumpy, but it's worth it. In designing a physical interface, it's crucial to understand how pixels relate to physical size. As it turns out, pixels probably aren't what you think they are.

CECI N'EST PAS UN PIXEL (THE TREACHERY OF VIEWPORTS)

Pixels ain't what they used to be. You're probably familiar with the pixel's original meaning as a physical dot on the screen. We call such pixels *hardware pixels,* and in the web's early days, these dots were the same size across all displays (96 dpi), because screens—and screen density—seldom changed. Now displays veer from very low-density screens on older devices to the super-dense Retina display and its ilk. This diversity created a problem for legacy web pages designed in pixels: a site on a high-resolution screen rendered much smaller in physical size than on a low-resolution screen (**FIG 2.7**).

To shore up this problem, the W3C redefined the pixel in 2011 with CSS 2.1. The new pixel was no longer a hardware-dependent speck of light, but instead referred to a precise physical distance. We diverged, in other words, from hardware pixels into so-called *virtual pixels,* sometimes known as *reference pixels, CSS pixels,* or *web pixels.* These virtual pixels have a specific size, just like an inch or a centimeter, that remains the same across hardware, no matter what its hardware pixel density.

The W3C locked in the pixel at 96 dpi, the legacy size of ye olde desktop monitors—or 1/96 inches. This approach would have made things nice and tidy...had browsers actually followed the standard. Trouble is, touchscreen browsers don't hew to this 96 dpi virtual pixel. In fact, phone and tablet browsers work as well as they do only because they willfully ignore the rule.

FIG 2.7: Varying screen resolutions introduced a problem of scale: the same content (say, an image file) appeared at a different physical size on high-resolution screens (left) vs. low-resolution ones (right). A pixel was no longer the same size across devices. Photograph by Veronika Sky Kindred (http://bkaprt.com/dft/02-07/).

Dynamic viewports demand dynamic pixels

The culprit is the *dynamic viewport,* the bit of magic that lets you pinch and zoom into web pages. On these gadgets, websites (and thus pixels) have no specific physical size. Right now I'm looking at the *New York Times* website, which is 972 pixels wide as I write. According to the CSS spec, which equates 96 pixels with one inch, the site should be over 10″ wide:

```
972px ÷ 96dpi = 10.13"
```

Yet when I look at it on my phone, it's squeezed into less than 3 inches. And that's a good thing—the only way I can take in the whole page on a small screen. From there, I can zoom in to read it at a size that's suddenly much larger (**FIG 2.8**). That's what

FIG 2.8: The idea of a fixed-size pixel collapses when you zoom in and out of a website.

makes "desktop" websites usable on small screens. By design, dynamic viewports dismantle the idea of mapping a pixel to a fixed physical size.

The solution is to tell the viewport not to be dynamic. While a dynamic viewport is necessary for zooming in and out of a one-size-fits-all site, an even better answer is to size the website responsively to the device, so that zooming is rarely required.

Set the viewport size to device-width

Well-behaved responsive sites fix the viewport to the device width by adding this tag to a page's `<head>`:

```
<meta name="viewport" content="width=device-width,
    initial-scale=1.0" />
```

This says to the browser, *"I trust you to do the right thing; choose your own fixed width for my website."* Consider `device-width` to be a gadget's "natural" size in virtual pixels. On phones and tablets, that's the full width of the screen; on the desktop, it's the width of the browser window.

(As you might expect, `width=device-width` sets the viewport width. `initial-scale=1.0` tells the browser not to zoom the page up or down on page load. This has the happy side effect of preventing Mobile Safari from scaling the page up in landscape orientation. Instead, it reflows the landscape layout to fit the wider screen.)

Let's look at iPhone 6 to see how this works in practice. The phone's `device-width` is 375 pixels. (Again, these are virtual pixels, not hardware pixels; the high-resolution iPhone 6 is 750 hardware pixels wide.) When you use the `<meta>` tag shown above, that fixes the viewport size to this "natural" 375 web pixels. This also becomes the size that viewport media queries latch onto. In our iPhone 6 example, with this `<meta>` tag in place, any media query with a `max-width` or `min-width` that matches a `375px` viewport width will apply its CSS rules to the phone.

So on individual devices at least, web pixels can have a fixed width, assuming you set the viewport to the device width as shown above. But it's almost never the 96-dpi size that the original web specification says it should be. Apple's decision in 2007 to set the original iPhone's `device-width` to `320px` made its web pixels roughly 160 dpi, and that choice affected all the mobile browsers that followed: Apple made dynamic viewports a hit and also introduced the `<meta name="viewport">` tag, and everyone else followed suit. Nearly all mobile browsers now report a `device-width` that sizes virtual pixels at roughly the same pixel density: *160 dpi is the de facto standard for touchscreen web pixels.* And that's why the 44-pixel rule works.

Still with me? We've redefined the meaning of "pixel" several times in a couple of pages, but these gymnastics have landed us on a reliable metric for tap targets, based on the 160 dpi convention for touchscreen browsers. Maybe the screen isn't so unreliable—with a shift in perspective. The next chapter asks for a similar adjustment, but zooms in to focus on common interactions, rethinking design patterns to make them efficient for slow-moving fingers and thumbs. Start your engines, it's time to feed our need for speed.

3 FASTER FINGERS

THE BEST INTERFACES seem to translate intent into action instantly—a touch and it's done. Slicing moments and carving microseconds might not seem like a big deal, but those moments add up. Crucially, that efficiency imbues your interface with free-flowing zen. "It's funny that saving one second, or a tap, or a moment's thought actually matters, but it does," writes designer John McWade. "It makes the device transparent; it becomes less a machine and more an extension of the mind and hand. Just kind of wish, *whoosh,* and stuff happens, like it's alive, almost like it's breathing" (http://bkaprt.com/dft/03-01/).

The secret to this effortless UI? Build for comfort *and* speed. So far we've focused on comfort: good ergonomics and ample touch targets. But what does it take to make your interface *fast?* Normally when we talk speed, we talk technical performance—how long it takes to download and render a web page or app view. That's important, of course, but this focus on fast bytes ignores how we might speed up fingers and thumbs too. Many of the best practices we've inherited from the desktop era are out of touch with touch. This chapter shows you how to turbocharge those familiar design solutions for faster fingers.

You know those medical dramas, where the surgeon is backed by a heroic team of intuitive assistants who anticipate the doctor's every need, handing her the right instrument at just the right moment? That's the role model for your interface: standing quietly out of the way until needed and then appearing with exactly the tool that's required. The crux of providing fast interfaces is providing *just enough at just the right moment.*

Enable primary tasks directly from list views

We speed through tasks when we move through *less* UI: we absorb a page quickly when it focuses on only a few key tasks or information types, and we grok a single page faster than multiple pages. A screen that lists products, for example, should make it simple to add those products to the shopping cart from that screen (**FIG 3.1**). *Give people easy access to common single-tap actions* to let them motor through a list and dispatch items without switching views.

You don't have to burn pixel real estate to add these actions, either. You can treat these shortcuts as power-user options by spiriting them behind hidden panels and revealing them with a gesture (**FIG 3.2**). Many apps, including browsers, similarly show a contextual menu with a long press on any item. The downside is that these shortcuts are effectively invisible until discovered. We'll cover how to cue gestures in Chapter 5.

Offer just enough summary information

The principle about providing access to key tasks from list views also applies to key info. For instance, in a view that shows a list, embed the most important data for each item in that view, instead of asking people to drill into a series of separate *detail*

FIG 3.1: Need SPAM in a hurry? The FreshDirect grocery-shopping app gives a one-tap option to add a product to your cart. Tapping elsewhere in the row takes you to a detail screen with the skinny on your favorite potted meat.

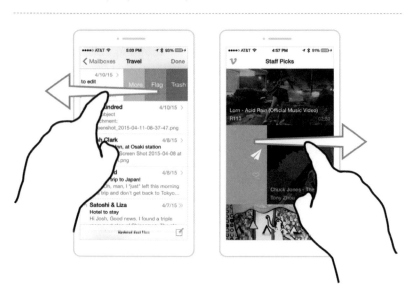

FIG 3.2: The Mail app in iOS (left) reveals a menu of options by swiping right to left across a message. Similarly, the Vimeo app for iPhone (right) lets you share or favorite a video by swiping left to right across it. Both actions save a trip to a separate screen.

FIG 3.3: This hourly view of the weather gives an at-a-glance forecast. Tap an hour for more details, but in most cases the temperature and weather icon is all you need.

screens. (It's in the name: reserve nice-to-know information—or plain details—for the detail view.) Telegraph the gotta-know info in the top-level list, and you short-circuit the need to ask for more. That's why email apps include the first several words of each message in the inbox view, letting you skim the list. Or take weather apps, which represent hourly or daily weather conditions with a familiar combo of temperature and ☀ ☁ icons. In most cases, this compact presentation is all people want in a forecast. Specifics about precipitation, barometric pressure, and other nitty-gritty niceties can—and should—be tucked a tap away for the curious, but the main use case is handled in the list view (**FIG 3.3**).

This approach is dubbed *progressive disclosure,* giving just enough information in the moment and offering more detail only upon request. Done right, progressive disclosure lets you keep the moment-to-moment experience clear and focused, while also giving access to complex data. To stick with our weather example, the best apps and sites let meteorology enthusiasts luxuriate in barometric stats while the rest of us can quickly check if we need an umbrella.

Progressive disclosure favors clarity over density, so the trade-off is that you add extra taps to access the most detailed information. That's okay. Creating faster interfaces isn't always about reducing the number of interactions; it's the quality that counts.

Distinguish quality taps from garbage taps

We're squeamish about extra taps and clicks, and with good reason; in the web's early years, slow network speeds meant it could take forever to find out what was on the other side of a link. That problem has returned with slow mobile networks, but we've learned a lot since the bad old days. Web pages can prefetch content before displaying it, and apps often have content ready in a local database. When network downloads aren't an issue, extra taps are often desirable, distilling each screen to a core message or task.

Tap quality is far more important than tap quantity. As long as each tap delivers *something*—new info, a completed task, or even a smile—that's a quality tap that maintains momentum. The enemy is a garbage tap, or any interaction you can avoid with a more thoughtful display of content or a more efficient gesture. Consider that weather report. If the hourly selector showed only the hours, with no temperature or weather icon, you'd have to tap every hour to see the day's evolving forecast— garbage taps. The simple addition of *just enough information* saves you from a dumpster dive.

Let user cues trigger the display of controls

Create interfaces that quietly watch (and react to) how people use them; let your app swoop in at the right time to present relevant options on a silver platter. This kind of *predictive interaction* doesn't require a fortune teller. In many cases, certain commands make sense only in certain contexts. Touch interfaces surface copy and paste tools, for example, only when you first

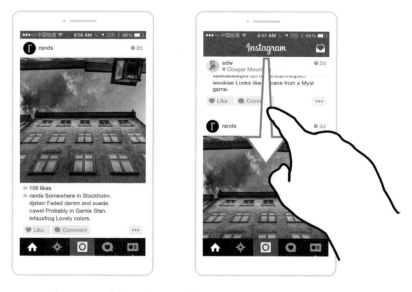

FIG 3.4: After you scroll down the page (left), the Instagram toolbar reappears when you scroll back up (right), anticipating that you might want the app's inbox menu.

select text. Other behavioral cues can tip you off to common wants: in Instagram, the river of photos flows down-screen and people almost always scroll down with that flow; scrolling up indicates a change in purpose. When that happens, Instagram guesses that you might be looking for the top-of-page controls and it slides them down into view (**FIG 3.4**).

The Instagram example shows prompt, thoughtful service, but it's also a shortcut for one of the most time-consuming interactions: the deadly long scroll. Instagram saves us a trip back to the top of a long page, but another solution is trimming the length in the first place.

WHITTLING DOWN THE LONG SCROLL

Scrolling in itself is not a bad thing—flicking through screens is part of a touchscreen's charm—but very long screens pose the

FIG 3.5: A wide screen (top) can present all columns at once, while smaller screens might display them as offscreen elements, displaying conceptually adjacent content when relevant or requested.

double downside of wearing out your thumb and your patience. Compact pages are touch-friendly pages.

The long scroll is common in small screens, where designers tend to stack content in a single interminable column. It's an understandable but ultimately lazy approach to responsive design: *What do I do with this three-column layout? Easy, I'll just stack 'em up into one awesomely gigantic column, and I'm done!* Even if your visitors make it all the way to the misbegotten content at page bottom, it's not clear their thumbs will have the strength to open it after all that swiping.

Managing lots of content requires more nuance. One strategy is to deploy *off-canvas layouts* (http://bkaprt.com/dft/03-02/). These layouts stash columns or content panels off screen until requested, another form of progressive disclosure (**FIG 3.5**). Some examples:

FIG 3.6: Many sites use a carousel to showcase a miscellaneous assortment of features. Unfortunately, this approach often hides the very content it seeks to highlight.

- A navigation menu that slides in from the top or side
- A sidebar that flies in with additional information
- A lengthy form that's divided into sections (large screens might display the entire form, while small screens display it section by section, each one sliding in as its own screen)

The off-canvas approach lets you to maintain a key feature of columns: displaying related content pieces adjacent to one another. Push a sidebar offscreen until relevant or requested, and you banish the long scroll while still keeping that related content right next door. Accordions, toggles, and other design patterns that compress secondary content do a similar service.

A popular but often misused off-canvas layout is the carousel. A *carousel* is a slideshow-style widget that slices content into individual panels, and you swipe or tap through those panels one by one (**FIG 3.6**). Its big draw is how it reduces a page's height by concentrating featured content into an island of horizontal panels. Despite good intentions, carousels often look for love in all the wrong places.

THE USE AND ABUSE OF CAROUSELS

Carousels can be terrific in the right contexts—we'll explore those in a bit—but they go awry in ill-considered ones, especially the homepage. Designers love homepage carousels because they seem to solve lots of problems by delivering high-impact visuals without sacrificing screen space. Media websites pour featured stories into carousels, and presto, all headlines magically share the same premium top-of-page position. Commerce sites do the same for promoted deals. Carousels even dangle the promise of slaying the designer's nemesis, organizational jockeying: on a company's marketing site, every department nabs a primo spot on the homepage—toss 'em into the carousel, job done.

If carousels offer compact display, visual impact, and a political dodge, then somebody let me onto this merry-go-round, right? Unfortunately, carousels are more fool's gold than silver bullet, because they demand those rarest of commodities: patience and attention.

A long haul

When the goal is to optimize click-throughs or fast page scans, carousels let us down. Consider a carousel promoting ten stories on a news site; landing on that tenth story demands a nine-swipe slog through the others—nine interactions before you ever see the headline. The story is ostensibly one of the day's most interesting, but it's buried under a pile of taps and swipes. A tool intended to feature content shouldn't hide it or give you thumb sprain to find it. The problem becomes worse when the carousel is a hodgepodge of features or products. When there's no organizing relationship to the collection, people don't know what's next in the carousel and lose interest.

One study found that 84% of click-throughs on a homepage carousel are on the first slide; the remaining slides see barely any action (http://bkaprt.com/dft/03-03/). See also "Auto-Forwarding Carousels, Accordions Annoy Users and Reduce Visibility" (http://bkaprt.com/dft/03-04/) and "Are Homepage Carousels Effective?"(http://bkaprt.com/dft/03-05/). There must be a better way to drive content to top-priority pages.

What about auto-advance? If people won't spin through every slide, let's do it for them. But the idea that anyone would sit still to watch a carousel advance is optimistic at best—especially in a mobile context. The tough truth is that you're asking the user to shoulder a decision and effort that belongs to you.

Force an editorial decision. The homepage carousel's siren song says nobody has to choose a single top story or product. *They're all featured!* It doesn't hold up in practice. If the overwhelming majority of people visit only the first item in a carousel, you can't pretend that you're equally featuring the others. Better to make an editorial choice, and highlight that single item in a way that also gives easier access to the secondary items.

Favor single-tap interactions. Instead of hiding featured content behind a slew of swipes, offer a single button to reveal everything at once. *Entertainment Weekly's* mobile homepage displays one primary feature and two secondary stories. Tap a More button, and you get twelve more headlines (**FIG 3.7**). This approach skips the fourteen *(fourteen!)* swipes you'd need to reach that last story in a carousel—zipping you there in one tap. Those twelve stories are still hidden behind the button, but the visible three stories hint at what you'll find on the other side. They replace the queasy smell of mystery meat with the reassuring scent of *information,* the confidence that you're on the right path to your goal.

Pack those panels. The *Entertainment Weekly* example works because it gives people *just enough summary information* to understand what's behind the More button, the key to any progressive-disclosure strategy. When you show several items on a single panel of a carousel, the resulting content density hints at what's likely on the next panel: a theme begins to emerge (**FIG 3.8**). This density also gives you a speed win by demanding fewer taps or swipes than single-item panels.

FIG 3.7: *Entertainment Weekly*'s mobile site reveals its top fifteen stories with a single interaction (tap the More Featured News button) instead of the fourteen swipes a carousel would require.

FIG 3.8: News homepages like *TechCrunch* and the *New York Times* deploy a mid-page carousel that shows several feature stories before inviting you to swipe for more.

When carousels are awesome

We've focused on the most egregious case—carousels as a homepage slideshow of miscellaneous content—but earlier I promised the right contexts for rolling out a carousel.

Carousels shine at linear data. Let's return to our hour-by-hour weather forecast. The carousel's horizontal presentation jibes with a typical timeline visualization, and because the order of the data is obvious and predictable, the scent of information is strong. You know what you'll get when you flick ahead: the next few hours of forecasts. But linear data doesn't have to be so stat-driven. Carousels also work well for PowerPoint-style slide shows that tell a yarn, make an argument, or provide a product tour; any logical progression of content is an array of linear data and a good carousel candidate (**FIG 3.9**).

Carousels are good for casual browsing of like items. Carousels are an apt format for photo galleries and slide shows, creating an environment for serendipitous discovery. As always, carousels work best when people have a solid sense of exactly

FIG 3.9: The site Should I Use a Carousel? (http://bkaprt.com/dft/03-06/) makes the case that carousels are evil. Ironically enough, its PowerPoint-style slide show is an excellent use of carousel as narrative.

what they'll encounter—which means the most effective slide shows zero in on a specific topic (red-carpet photos! cats in funny hats!). In this context, you're not optimizing for speed but a languorous stroll through the images, so the swipe-swipe-swipe of the carousel becomes a feature, not a bug.

BE RUTHLESS WITH FORM FIELDS

Web forms are the dreary administrivia we plod through to get the shiny thing we want: a service to receive, a product to buy. Forms are necessary hurdles, but the bigger the obstacle, the less shiny the thing on the other side seems. Twenty-one percent of abandoned shopping carts are left behind because customers say the process took too long (http://bkaprt.com/dft/03-07/). Every field matters: one study found that reducing a contact form from four fields to three improved conversion rates by *almost half* (http://bkaprt.com/dft/03-08/). Trimming

FIG 3.10: Nothing says "I love you" like filling out forty form fields at checkout.

FIG 3.11: Stop playing the field(s). You don't need three fields to ask for a name—or mercy, *nine fields* to ask for phone info.

the length of form fields is good practice for any platform, but it's crucial for touchscreens. For all of touch's many conveniences, precision interactions like typing and filling forms are not among them.

Kay Jewelers' mobile website asks customers to fill out forty fields during checkout (**FIG 3.10**). ("She's not worth it!" someone shouted when I once shared this form at a design workshop.) I'm not picking on Kay Jewelers; forty (or up!) is an unfortunately common number. Let's go prune some form fields.

Collapse multifield data. The form splits the customer's name into three fields: first, middle, last. It does the same for phone numbers and the street address (**FIG 3.11**).

All three cases should squeeze into single fields. Too many forms present a one-to-one relationship between the form and the site's database. If a database has three fields for a name, the

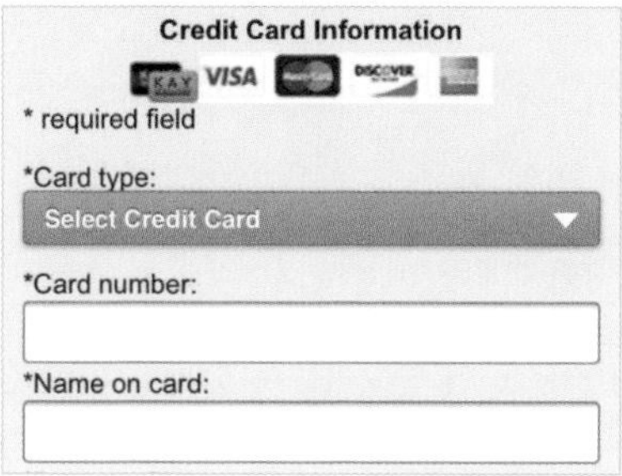

FIG 3.12: No need to ask customers for credit card type; it's embedded in the card number.

designer dutifully carries those fields over. But it's not your customer's job to fill in your database; you should do some of that work for them. Every move to a new field requires yet another tap and a break in flow. Ease people's way by collapsing multifield data into one field, and do the parsing on the backend to split that information for your database.

Don't ask for unnecessary info. Any additional field is a burden on your customer. Our example form asks for not one but three phone numbers. Asking for even one is of dubious value for online purchases; do you really need two more? Do you need a full billing address, when most credit card processors require only a postal code? Be ruthless about the amount of information you request.

Answer your own questions. Related, don't ask customers questions you can answer yourself. No need to ask for city and state/region if you have the postal code. No need to ask what type of credit card they've provided, since that's embedded in the account number. (American Express cards start with either 34 or 37, for example; MasterCards begin with 51 to 55.) Again, don't make your customer fill in the database.

Simplify for credit cards. Most card processors require very little for authentication: account number, expiration date, security code (CVV, the card verification value), and postal code. This is all numeric data. Mobile payment service Square pioneered the clever fix of collapsing that information into a single input field, and gives you a numeric keypad to fly through the data entry (**FIG 3.13**).

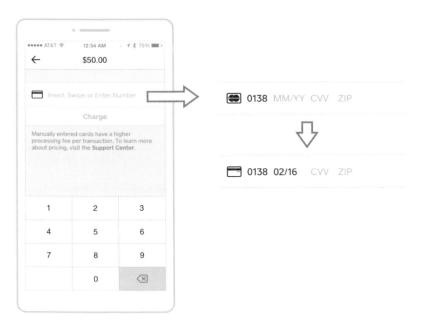

FIG 3.13: Square lets you fill in credit card details in a single field using just a numeric keyboard. As you fill in the data, the field's icon morphs to confirm the card type (top right) and show you where to find the security code, or CVV (bottom right).

You begin by entering your credit card; as you type the first few digits, the credit card image changes per the type of card. When you finish entering the number, the string shortens to the last four digits and the input field transforms to display the remaining three bits of required info: expiration date, CVV, and zip code. No need to switch fields, just motor through the data, tapping numbers on the keypad. When you get to the CVV, the credit card image even flips and highlights where you can find the card's security code. The pattern saves time, taps, and screen space while offering guidance and verification as you go.

Inspired by Square's approach, developer Zachary Forrest crafted an HTML prototype to make it available for the web (http://bkaprt.com/dft/03-09/).

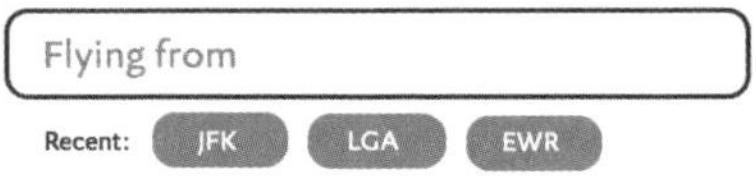

FIG 3.14: Offer best-guess suggestions for single-tap data entry.

DO YOU REALLY NEED THAT KEYBOARD?

Implicit in this imperative to slash forms is that typing on touchscreens is just...so...slow. Don't get me wrong, we'll do it with proper motivation. A popular myth holds we aren't willing to type on touchscreens, but we send and receive an average of thirty-five text messages per day (http://bkaprt.com/dft/03-10/)—and over one hundred for teens (http://bkaprt.com/dft/03-11/). That doesn't mean we're great at it. Touchscreen typing is still error-prone. Whenever you're tempted to bring up the keyboard, first consider the alternatives.

Supplement text fields with single-tap alternatives. If the odds are good that someone will enter one of a handful of values, offer single-tap buttons for those values alongside the field. For example, a travel site might use a customer's purchase history or GPS location to suggest airport codes for departure airports (**FIG 3.14**).

Support autofill. Most browsers offer *autofill,* the ability to fill out a form with common information like name, address, phone, email, and so on. Help browsers grab the right fields by using specific values in the name and autocomplete attributes of those inputs (**FIG 3.15**). Like so:

```
<form method=”post” autocomplete=”on”>
  Name: <input type=”text” name=”name”
  autocomplete=”name”>
  Email: <input type=”email” name=”email”
  autocomplete=”email”>
  Phone: <input type=”tel” name=”phone”
  autocomplete=”tel”>
  Address: <input type=”text” name=”address”
  autocomplete=”address”>
</form>
```

CONTENT TYPE	name	autocomplete
Name	name fname mname lname	name
Email	email	email
Address	address city region province state zip zip2 postal country	street-address locality region postal-code country
Phone	phone mobile country-code area-code exchange suffix ext	tel
Credit Card	ccname cardnumber cvc ccmonth ccyear exp-date card-type	cc-name cc-number cc-csc cc-exp-month cc-exp-year cc-exp cc-type

FIG 3.15: Recommended name and autocomplete values.

You can specify whether a form allows autofill by setting autocomplete="on" on form or input fields (autofill only works when the form's method attribute is set to post). By default, forms always accept autofill, but users may need to turn on autofill itself in their browser preferences.

Use data from other apps. The info you're asking for may already be on the device. If you're designing an app with access to the address book, let someone choose a contact to autofill address, phone, and email. In the example of the travel app, a "Flying to" field could offer to select a contact to get the address of your destination, fetching the closest airport and, if applicable, local travel options to take you the rest of the way (e.g., rental car, train, or bus).

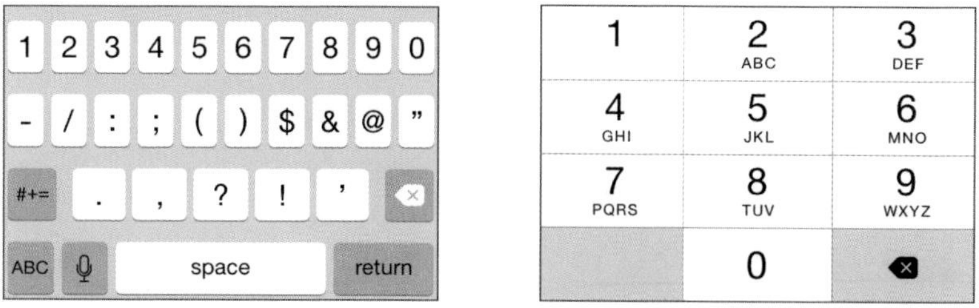

FIG 3.16: Ask mobile Safari for a simple `type="number"` field and you get a keyboard jammed with punctuation options (left). Adding `pattern` and `inputtype` attributes, however, gives you an all-numbers keypad (right).

THE RIGHT KEYBOARD FOR THE RIGHT JOB

When you've gotta go keyboard, outfit people with the appropriate keyboard by paying attention to the `type` attribute of a web page's `input` elements. Most touchscreen browsers offer optimized keyboards for these input types to fly through forms:

```
<input type="email">
<input type="url">
<input type="tel">
<input type="number">
```

In most browsers, those `type` attributes trigger exactly the keyboard you'd expect. In mobile Safari, though, the `type="number"` keyboard displays both numbers and punctuation (**FIG 3.16**). If you want a numeric keypad, you can force it by specifying a `pattern` attribute and throwing in `inputtype` for good measure:

```
<input type="number" pattern="[0-9]*"
  inputtype="numeric">
```

Many touch browsers also use `type` to sidestep the keyboard entirely for date- or time-based inputs. Use one of these input types to get a native date- or time-picker control (**FIG 3.17**).

FIG 3.17: Android Chrome (left) displays a full-screen calendar UI when you tap into an `<input type="date">` field, while mobile Safari (right) shows a somewhat homely three-spinner date picker.

```
<input type="date">
<input type="time">
<input type="datetime">
<input type="month">
```

Date pickers are fine if you're prompting any arbitrary date over a large time span (like a birthday), but better and faster options exist if you want dates in a more limited range. We'll look at an example in a moment, but the reason to be skeptical of spinner-style date pickers is they're fussy to use on touch-screens. That's why the `select` element is next on our hit list.

In desktop interfaces, `select`'s dropdown menu is a stalwart of information density, packing potentially hundreds of preformatted options into one compact control. That's a *visual* savings, however; in touch, a select menu tends to waste both time and taps. It takes two taps just to summon and dismiss the menu, followed by several swipes and some fine-tuning to make the selection. It's a touch-hostile experience.

Replace long menus with type-ahead suggestions. Consider a select menu for the fifty US states. Poor Wyoming stakes out the lonely end of that alphabetical list, putting it many, many swipes away for touch users. (Wisconsin, next to last, is even harder to hit; with Wyoming, you can at least slam into the bottom of the spinner and stop. With Wisconsin, you have to nudge the menu to nab it.) It's far faster to tap on a text field and start typing, letting the interface make suggestions as you go (**FIG 3.18**). Four taps whisk you to Wyoming: select the field, type *W*, type *Y*, tap the suggested *Wyoming*, and you're done.

In theory, HTML5's `datalist` element makes it easy to incorporate type-ahead suggestions; `datalist` looks like a plain input element on the page, but it lets the website supply a set of data suggestions. You do this by associating an input field with a `datalist` element via the `list` attribute:

```
<input id="state" list="state-list">
<datalist id="state-list">
  <option value="Vermont">
  <option value="Virginia">
  <option value="Washington">
  <option value="West Virginia">
  <option value="Wisconsin">
  <option value="Wyoming">
</datalist>
```

At this writing, however, browser support for `datalist` remains poor on mobile browsers, which fall back to text input fields, sans magical suggestion powers. While we wait for browser support to improve, you can get the same effect

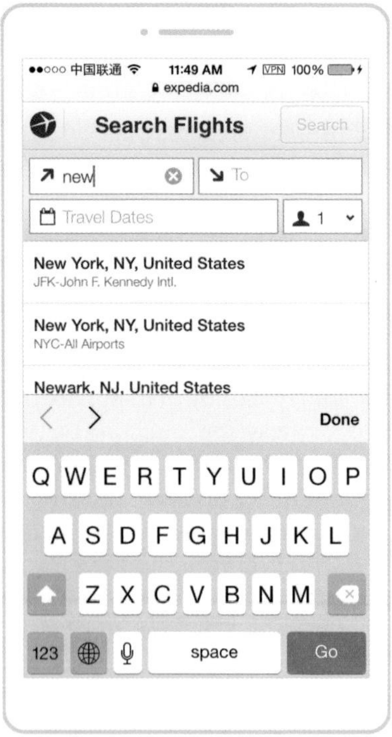

FIG 3.18: Expedia's website offers finger-friendly type-ahead options when entering departure and destination cities.

●●○○○ 中国联通 🛜   11:49 AM   ⌁ VPN 100% ▭▸
🔒 expedia.com

✈ **Search Flights**   Search

↗ new   ⊗   ↘ To

📅 Travel Dates   👤 1 ⌄

New York, NY, United States
JFK-John F. Kennedy Intl.

New York, NY, United States
NYC-All Airports

Newark, NJ, United States

‹ ›   **Done**

Q W E R T Y U I O P

A S D F G H J K L

⇧ Z X C V B N M ⌫

123 🌐 🎤   space   Go

in these browsers with a bit of JavaScript pixie dust. See Lea Verou's Awesomeplete library (http://bkaprt.com/dft/03-12/) and Mike Taylor's jQuery Datalist plugin (http://bkaprt.com/dft/03-13/) for two examples.

Replace short menus with single-tap options. When you're dealing with a small set of options, don't pack those items away in a menu. Expose them all to allow one-tap selection (**FIG 3.20**). This route yields a much faster experience for short date ranges than the aforementioned native date picker.

Use stepper buttons for small number ranges. If you're prompting for a number in a relatively narrow range (like for airplane or movie tickets), use plus and minus *stepper buttons*

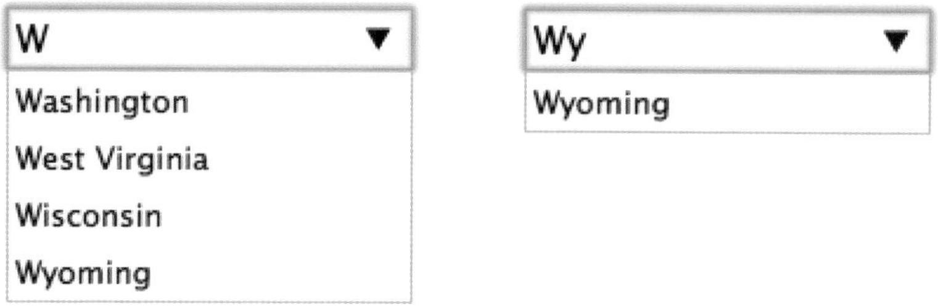

FIG 3.19: datalist gives you instant type-ahead suggestions.

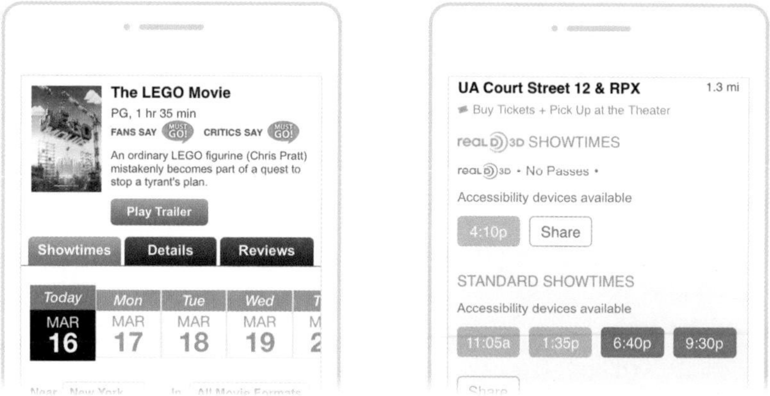

FIG 3.20: Fandango typically sells movie tickets only a few days in advance, making for a limited set of values. The website exposes those dates (left) for easy access instead of hiding them in a menu. Showtimes get a similar treatment (right).

to let people bump the number up or down with a single tap (FIG 3.21). Steppers are ideal when the values are likely to be adjusted only slightly.

We've tuned cases for hustling your visitors through form fields. There's one case, though, where forms are designed to slow people down—in a good way.

FIG 3.21: Fandango uses stepper buttons for fewer taps when selecting ticket quantities.

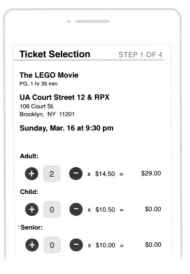

The LEGO Movie
PG, 1 hr 35 min

UA Court Street 12 & RPX
106 Court St.
Brooklyn, NY 11201

Sunday, Mar. 16 at 9:30 pm

Adult:

⊕ 2 ⊖ x $14.50 = $29.00

Child:

⊕ 0 ⊖ x $10.50 = $0.00

Senior:

⊕ 0 ⊖ x $10.00 = $0.00

FIGHT! GESTURE JIUJITSU VS OK | CANCEL

"Are you sure you want to delete this message?"
OK | Cancel
"Do you want to save changes?"
OK | Cancel
"Do you really think it's a good idea to eat that burrito?"
OK | Cancel

Despite their widespread use, *confirmation dialogs* are rarely effective. These alerts are meant to slow us down for a moment of reflection, but we've developed an immunity to them. Too easy to dismiss but too annoying to heed, they're irritating speed bumps that don't do their intended job.

Well-placed gestures provide this protection better and faster. Call it *gesture jiujitsu:* defensive fu with the flick of a finger. The swipe is a champ at this: swipe to unlock, swipe to answer a call, swipe to power off, swipe to delete. The gesture is just difficult enough to signal definite intent, but easy enough that it doesn't take you out of the flow of your activity. Instead

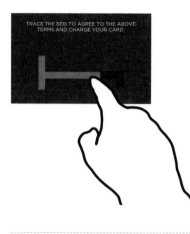

FIG 3.22: Hotel Tonight prompts customers to trace the logo to accept terms and conditions.

of a confirmation dialog, add a little gesture-defense to protect your users against actions they might regret. (Double-down with an even better tactic, *undo*. Wherever possible, let people take back that last action. Be forgiving of errors and let people get out of a jam with grace and ease.)

When you need even more user attention, crank up the complexity of the gesture. That's how hotel-reservation app Hotel Tonight presents its terms of use. The service specializes in last-minute reservations, which means bookings are non-refundable, an urgent fact for customers to understand. To make sure, the app asks you to complete a simple gesture—trace the company's bed-shaped logo—to confirm (**FIG 3.22**).

THE HANDS-FREE INTERFACE

Aside from gesture jujitsu, most of the improvements we've looked at pare interactions down, creating touch interfaces that require, well, less touch. For all of touchscreens' promise, they're clumsy, slow, or imprecise for some tasks, and no amount of UI optimization will fix that completely. Better in those cases to opt for a non-touch alternative, a lesson the Ford Motor Company learned when they replaced their knobs-and-buttons dashboard with a touchscreen version.

Customers rightfully complained it became too difficult—and dangerous!—to switch radio stations or change the volume while behind the wheel. Driving is one of many contexts where touch is a poor interactive solution—because your eyes aren't available to look at the screen. Unlike with mechanical controls, you can't feel your way through a glass-slab interface. Give a driver a touchscreen, and you give them an accident waiting to happen. Ford should've known better, and in the end, they did: they brought back traditional knobs and buttons (http://bkaprt.com/dft/03-14/).

Physical controls are one answer, but other options have emerged. Sensor-laden devices give us the chance to forgo tapping from the start, pushing the interaction off the screen and into our environment. GPS-location sensors inspired the first wave of sensor-based design, with websites and apps that tell us where to get the nearest cup of coffee or when the next train is leaving from the closest station. Figuring out what's nearby was a game-changing trick. But now sensors can do something even more powerful: figure out what's right in front of you.

That idea propels the homely bar code and its younger (and less popular) cousin, the QR code. When you encode data like a URL into those lines and dots, and then let the camera read it for you, you eliminate work for your fingers and thumbs. But camera vision has become far more sophisticated than that, enabling potent shortcuts:

- When you create an account with eBay's app, you can skip entering your name and address by scanning your driver's license with your camera; the app reads your info and completes the form for you.
- Mobile Safari on iOS fills out payment info when you take a photo of your credit card.
- Use the Google Translate app to point your camera at text in one language, and it automatically converts the text to another (FIG 3.24). The app displays the translation in real time, in the same typeface and color, right on your screen, as if you were peering through a magically multilingual window.

FIG 3.23: Google Translate's "word lens" provides live translation using the camera and old-school optical character recognition. It saves the effort of typing (and mistyping) an unfamiliar language into a form. Video image from Google (http://bkaprt.com/dft/03-16/).

- Layar is a web service and mobile app that enables editors to embed digital multimedia in printed pages. Snap a photo of a magazine layout, and the page springs to life with video and related links.
- People with no or low vision can use the LookTel Money Reader app to identify the denomination of currency. In the US, it's impossible to differentiate between bills without sight; phones now provide vision for those who don't have it. When sensors supplement a touchscreen, devices can provide astonishingly good interfaces for people with poor sight or other disabilities. For more examples, see "Visually Impaired Turn to Smartphones to See Their World" (http://bkaprt.com/dft/03-15/).

And that's only the camera. Today's gadgets are packed with other sensor-enabled superpowers:

- Microphones let devices hear. Check out the Web Audio API (http://bkaprt.com/dft/03-17/) to learn more about how browsers can make and recognize sounds. The Web Speech

API (http://bkaprt.com/dft/03-18/) similarly lets browsers understand and speak words.

- GPS notes your location and, better, what's nearby. The Geolocation API (http://bkaprt.com/dft/03-19/) gives browsers the 411.
- Fingerprint readers provide instant ID.
- Accelerometers, gyroscopes, and the compass track motion and activity. The Device Orientation API (http://bkaprt.com/dft/03-20/) helps browsers figure out which way is up.
- Light sensors tell browsers when it's light or dark via the Ambient Light API (http://bkaprt.com/dft/03-21/).

Add standard networking via Wi-Fi, cellular service, Bluetooth, and NFC, and gadgets can socialize with one another, as either data sources or remote-controlled interfaces. As tiny networked computers get embedded in more and more objects, places, and appliances, the amount of ambient data that our personal devices can access and manipulate will multiply. Always think: How might you gather and use that data in ways that can save people time, effort—or the dreary work of data entry?

In other words: *How can you deliver the maximum results for the minimum input?* These sensor-based examples offer more than fast shortcuts for input; more important—and more interesting—they take their cues directly from a person's environment. When we design for sensors, not just screens, the whole world becomes a digital canvas. As users, that gives us the chance to interact more directly with the people and places we truly care about, restoring some of the attention we've ceded to screens.

Screens aren't done yet, though. As an industry, we're just beginning to explore the potential of touch-enabled interfaces and the ability to swipe, pinch, and flick your way through information. Direct touch interaction lets us make information behave as physical object. When you embrace gestures, your interface becomes not only speedy but natural, obvious, and intuitive.

GESTURES

HANDS ARE WONDERFULLY EXPRESSIVE. We talk with our hands all the time: they ask questions, show intent, command attention, reveal emotion. A backhanded wave dismisses an idea; a jab of the finger accuses; a thumbs-up enthuses. If hands are excellent at communicating with people, they're even more effective at communicating with objects. From the delicate operation of tying a shoelace to the blunt-force strength of opening a pickle jar, our hands and fingers constantly improvise in grip, pressure, position, and sensitivity.

How can we bring similar expression to manipulating digital information? Touchscreens put data literally in the user's hands, and it's the designer's job to enable (and interpret) that interaction. Unfortunately, while our hands have a robust vocabulary for speaking to people and objects, we're still in the grammar-school stages of a gestural language for touchscreens. A richer lexicon lies ahead, but it will take time for a more sophisticated range of touchscreen gestures to become common knowledge.

This chapter explores the possibilities. We'll begin by looking at the handful of gestures that are already well understood. We'll see why traditional interface elements like buttons and tabs fall short of touch's expressive potential—and what makes for better alternatives. Along the way, we'll sidestep the gotchas of gesture design, and we'll wrap up with the techniques (and headaches) of coding gestures in the browser. But first, the fundamentals.

THE BASIC GESTURE VOCABULARY

A smattering of core gestures runs across platforms. These are the gestures that you can rely on people to understand and discover on their own. They're your gestural building blocks.

Tap

This is the click of the touch universe, the all-purpose action to interact with any screen element. Tap signals, "I want to learn more about this" or "I want to activate this." As discussed in Chapter 1, tap is also the best proxy for hover in a touch environment: use a tap to "peek" into an object, previewing info without opening a detail view; use a second tap to activate it.

Swipe

Like tap, swipe is so familiar that its uses seem both obvious and limited: swipe to scroll or switch between views. But subtler uses have crept in. Swipe reveals hidden panels, for example, like the cross-platform pattern to swipe from top for status-bar notifications, or the Windows edge gestures to slide out control panels. As we saw in the last chapter, swipe is also a crucial move in defensive design, preventing people from triggering actions they might later regret: swipe to unlock the phone, answer a call, or delete.

Long press

Akin to the right-click, the long press conjures a contextual menu of related actions or info about the touched item. This holds in spirit across all touch platforms, but the specifics vary:

- **Windows.** A long press here acts most like a mouse's right-click; it summons a contextual menu. (You can also trigger this menu in Windows with a two-finger tap: press with one finger and do a quick second tap with another.)
- **Android.** A long press on a list item brings up Android's *contextual action bar,* which lets you select additional items from the list, then take action on all of them at once (e.g., delete, move).
- **Web.** Most touch browsers use the long tap to trigger contextual menus for links and images (for actions like save, copy, share, etc.). That means if a web app wants to use the long press, it has to override default browser behavior—almost always bad for usability.
- **iOS.** iOS apps deploy the long press less consistently than these other platforms, though it still invokes a contextual menu or summary content. Its uneven use, however, means that the long press is typically discovered only by expert or curious users, so it's best to treat it as a shortcut alternative to visiting a detail screen.

Long press and drag

On all platforms, this triggers drag and drop behavior. A long press on a draggable item signals your intent to move it, and the drag carries it to its destination.

Pinch and spread

This duo typically shrinks and enlarges images, maps, and web pages. It's a pleasingly immediate interaction that lets you grab an object and then crunch or stretch it.

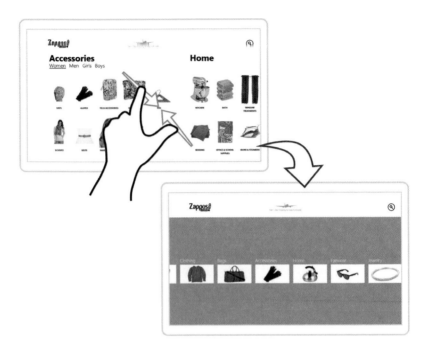

FIG 4.1: Pinch the browsing view of the Zappos app to trigger semantic zoom in Windows for a more visual overview of the store's departments.

This literal zoom effect is supplemented in a growing number of applications by a more metaphorical version called *semantic zoom*—an emerging convention thanks to its widespread use in Windows. There, semantic zoom zips between two views: a close-up and a bird's-eye perspective on the high-level organization. For example, in the Zappos shopping app for Windows, the zoomed view shows all the departments with their product categories: hats, gloves, etc., in Accessories (**FIG 4.1**). For faster scanning, pinch that view to pull back to a simplified list of the same departments without their categories. Spread or tap a department to zoom back in.

Other approaches extend semantic zoom to navigate more deeply into the information hierarchy. For example, Photos for iPad offers pinch and spread as an alternate way to navigate

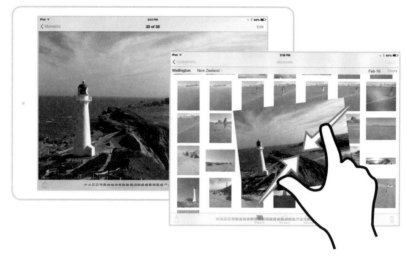

FIG 4.2: Pinch a photo in iPad's Photos app to close it and return to the parent album's thumbnail view. The gesture provides an alternative to tapping the Moments back button at top left.

between an album and individual photos (**FIG 4.2**). When you're admiring one of your pictures, you can tap the back button to return to a thumbnail view of all the photos in the album. But you can *also* pinch the screen to return to that thumbnail album view. Here semantic zoom is deployed to let you move up and down the app's organizational levels. Pinch a detail view (the photo) to close it and return to the level above (the album), or from the album view, spread a thumbnail image to open it to its detail view.

Double-tap

Like pinch and spread, double-tap zooms in and out. (Android adds nuance to double-tap zooming with double-tap and slide. When you slide up and down after a double-tap in Android, you can control the precise amount to zoom; sliding up zooms out and sliding down zooms in.) Double-tap has few conventional uses beyond zooming, however, making it ripe for experimentation in other contexts. BostonGlobe.com, for example, lets subscribers double-tap a headline to save the article for later reading. You can count on your audience to understand these six gestures without additional help. But while reliable, this kit remains primitive—it simply ports existing mouse-and-cursor interactions to the touchscreen. These gestures are exactly as expressive as a mouse cursor, reducing the hand's subtlety to a single jabbing finger. As a result, they tend to reinforce old, troubled desktop metaphors.

THE TROUBLE WITH BUTTONS

Buttons have served us well in both the physical and digital worlds, but their translation to touchscreens is more unwieldy: buttons take effort, add complexity, and insert an abstract layer between you and the content. Touch has the potential to sweep away the abundance of buttons, menus, folders, tabs, and administrative debris we've accumulated over decades of desktop computing. A new choreography of gestures can and should replace those timeworn controls to let us work directly with content.

Buttons take effort

Physical interfaces require physical effort. For small touch-screens, that effort is modest, usually only the sweep of a thumb. As screens get larger, however, the effort increases. Roaming the screen means shifting your whole hand, or even your arm, to work the controls. I know, I know—how hard is it to flip your hands across a screen? But fatigue sets in with time and repetition. A few years ago, I judged a digital magazine competition, poring over hundreds of iPad apps. After several hours of bad ergonomic designs, no kidding, my arms were sore from reaching over and over into the screen for basic navigation tasks. Call it *iPad elbow*.

Consider the Back button in the top left of many iPad apps. We're asked to hit it all the time—to go back, to browse an app's

FIG 4.3: The back button in Mail for iPad requires a slight reach (left), but the swipe gesture (right) lets you access the same content no matter where your hands sit.

hierarchy, and so on. The button is in the thumb zone, but it still takes a moment of concentration and effort to hit it. Despite the sweeping expanse of a tablet screen, this tiny patch of pixels demands constant attention.

On larger screens like tablets, favor coarse gestures over fine-tuned pecking. Let people paw at the whole screen for basic actions like simple navigation. In iPad's Mail app, for example, the Inbox back button opens the message drawer, but you can also pull it open by swiping left to right anywhere on the screen (**FIG 4.3**). The entire screen becomes the control—no special trip to the back button required.

Coarse gestures help reduce errors and improve accessibility. When Boeing designers asked me how they might make touch interfaces more forgiving of pilots' errant fingers during turbulence, I suggested using coarse gestures (a swipe, full-hand pinch, etc.) to let pilots slap at the screen instead of requiring careful button presses. The same advice holds for seniors, children, or others with limited motor control. Likewise, these gestures provide no-look control for those who have limited vision of the screen—like drivers and cyclists.

Big gestures also tend to develop into reflexes. Traditional interfaces rely on *visual memory,* asking us to scan buttons and labels to absorb their meaning. Touch interfaces ask some of the same, but blend in *muscle memory*—a subconscious knowledge of the interface that seems to spring right out of our hands and fingers. Like playing an instrument or typing a keyboard, the repetitive actions of working a touchscreen settle into instinct. Touchscreens depart from physical interfaces in an important way, though: their glass surfaces don't provide the physical feedback of an instrument's strings or a keyboard's buttons. Fine controls slow us down by demanding we *look* at the screen. Coarse gestures, however, quickly embed into muscle memory and require little visual processing; users of laptop trackpads think nothing of the two-finger gesture for scrolling, for example. Broad expressive actions make the best touch interfaces more like playing an instrument than using a push-button tool.

Buttons add complexity

We've all been baffled by the dense undergrowth of buttons that blanket our cars, home appliances, remote controls, and other everyday machinery. On a recent summer trip, my family counted over eighty buttons in our Citroën rental car; it took us ten minutes to figure out how to get the thing moving. (The Citroën C4 has a steering wheel with thirteen buttons and four scroll wheels—*scroll wheels!)* This complexity of common interfaces mirrors the growing complexity of the associated device, creating a familiar design challenge: more features seem to call for more controls. But if you're not careful, buttons start sprouting like mushrooms all over your interface.

Take a lesson from console gaming. What began as a single-button joystick in the first Atari games has evolved into elaborate, button-addled controllers. A standard Xbox One controller features eleven buttons, two triggers, two joysticks, and a D-pad. The first generation of iPhone games in 2008 ported over this button-based system, with awkward results (**FIG 4.4**). Onscreen buttons took up valuable space, obscured gameplay, and locked fingers and thumbs in place. They were hard to use too: since fingers skid across glass, virtual buttons lack the reassuring no-look feel of their physical counterparts. The buttons backfired.

Like many others, the game *Earthworm Jim* ported console-style controls to small-screen phones, choking out the actual gameplay.

Game designers needed a new model—so they ditched buttons. With fewer controls, game designers pared down features. Simple but satisfying games like *Angry Birds* ruled touchscreens with one or two gestures. *The nature of the game adapted to the nature of the input.* As gesture gaming found success, more sophisticated games developed to rival cinematic console games. Some, like the fantasy action game *Infinity Blade,* used gestures to drive familiar hack-and-slash games. Others took an even more novel approach, creating gameplay purpose-built for the touchscreen. Games like *République* (FIG 4.5) or *Monument Valley* invite you to tap inside the game environment to move the game's hero. Instead of depending on complex button-based puppetry, they draw you in by interacting directly with the game world. It's a shift in perspective that delivers the complex experience of a console game without the need for correspondingly complex controls.

All software genres should explore a similar perspective shift, embracing more direct interaction and fewer buttons and controls. It's worth acknowledging that touching a button is a

FIG 4.5: In *République,* you're a hacker who guides the hero to escape from a mysterious facility. You view the world through surveillance cameras and tell her where to go and when to move. Most actions involve tapping on cameras to take them over, and then tapping on locations to tell the escapee where to go. The world itself is the control, no buttons required.

kind of direct interaction. The trouble is that this connection is with a *button,* not the information you seek to manipulate. Or, put another way...

Buttons are a hack

Don't get me wrong: hacks—and buttons—aren't all bad. We invented electrical switches and buttons over a century ago to control objects at a distance. These switches were designed as messengers to carry our intent (turn on the lights) to its destination (the lightbulb). While convenient, this interaction is also indirect, completely disconnected from the thing we want to affect. A light switch here for a lightbulb over there isn't obvious; it has to be discovered, learned. When I'm in a new hotel room, it takes me a minute or two of trying switches to figure out how to turn on that one light. But that's far better than stumbling into a dark room with a ladder and climbing up to screw in a bulb. The light switch is an inspired hack. When it's not convenient to interact with the primary object, adding a control to work it from a distance is ingenious. *Buttons are workarounds for moments direct interaction isn't possible.* It's a similar story for buttons in virtual interfaces. We created buttons and tabs and sliders as skeuomorphic intermediaries to work with digital information and actions that were beyond reach or easy representation. Buttons still have their place, and their obvious labels and clear calls to action make them especially useful. Embrace them as needed, but recognize that they remain workarounds. Every time you add a button to your layout, challenge yourself: *can I find a way to manipulate content more directly?*

Information as physical object

Every digital interface is an illusion, a thin layer of magic atop a churn of ones and zeroes. For the first time, though, touchscreens present the opportunity to create *the illusion that there is no illusion,* that there's nothing between you and the content. This book has stressed the importance of physical interaction; to complete the illusion, let's now apply that same thinking to the data itself.

Reimagine your information as a physical object. Ask this of every element of your interface: "What could I do with this piece of data if I could slide, stretch, and poke at it under glass?" Semantic zoom—bestowing pinch-to-zoom physicality on the underlying information architecture—is one example. Now consider how you might select a date range. A typical design uses two calendar-style date pickers, a solution that does use physical metaphor by riffing on paper calendars. But that doesn't imbue data with physical properties and direct interaction. Instead, imagine *the date range itself* as an object with mass and elasticity—stretch or squeeze its ends to make it the size you want (**FIG 4.6**).

Make content the control

This reimagining helps clear away as much interface as possible between the user and the content. All UI is social conven-

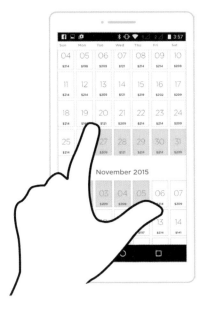

FIG 4.6: Imagine a date range as a rubber band whose endpoints you can squeeze or stretch to whatever size you want.

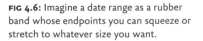

tion, and those conventions run into trouble when they're not evenly understood. In his book *Living with Complexity,* designer Don Norman notes the holes that distinguish salt and pepper shakers—and how people have decidedly mixed opinions on whether a single hole denotes salt or pepper. Norman points out that it doesn't really matter which is "correct." What matters is what the person who fills them believes. That would be fine if everyone understood the system the same way, but that's not the case. Even if I'm certain that salt should be in the shaker with one hole, I can't trust that others share that view; when I'm at a restaurant, I test by shaking a little into my hand first. I don't have confidence in the system.

As designers, we're the ones filling the shakers. Our job is to give users confidence. To do so, we often fall back to explicit labels for "salt" and "pepper." But that still requires visual processing (and command of English) to decipher each shaker. You know what's better? Glass bottles that let us see the salt and pepper inside, no reading or scanning of labels necessary, just grab what we need (**FIG 4.7**).

FIG 4.7: Guess which set of shakers is faster to figure out? Left photograph by Joe King (http://bkaprt.com/dft/04-01/); right photograph by Black Country Museums (http://bkaprt.com/dft/04-02/).

Touchscreen photo galleries are nearly perfect examples of this. They're very dense interfaces, yet with almost no controls. It's all content: tap a photo to make it bigger, then swipe through the collection. Interaction is tied entirely to the content; the information itself is the interface. Marshall McLuhan famously said, "The medium is the message." When we create the illusion of direct interaction with information, we can finally say that the message is the medium.

So what does interaction look like when we press this message under two-dimensional glass? In the physical world, we have a word for individual pieces of flat content; we call them *cards*. That's why all the major touch operating systems use cards (or tiles or panels) as their core metaphor for representing direct-interaction content.

The power of the card metaphor

Cards have become a popular way to represent individual data objects: a photo on Facebook, a flight from TripIt, a contact, a coupon, a Yelp review, a Google Now reminder, a game level, and so on (FIG 4.8). Until recently, we settled on sharing those chunks of information via URLs in email or text. Now, data cards provide a snack-sized, portable format that shuffles neatly into interlocking modules in big-screen responsive websites, or as the main event in small-screen apps. Plus, cards are fun:

FIG 4.8: Pinterest pins (left), TripIt (right), Google Now, Twitter cards—a variety of services embed cards as tiny multimedia canvases into apps, web pages, social streams, notification windows, and more.

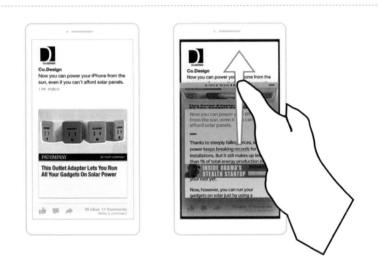

FIG 4.9: Facebook Paper imagines its data as a physical card, where every physical action has a corresponding data action. Web-headline cover cards unfold to reveal their interactive insides.

when we represent data objects like trading cards, business cards, or paper coupons, we have a natural and even nostalgic impulse to share and exchange them in the same way—collect 'em all!

Cards also suggest lots of physical interactions. The most basic and familiar, of course, is flipping. On phones, screens are stacked just like a deck of cards. You swipe back and forth through your browser history, flicking with your thumb as if you were dealing cards at your weekly canasta game—it's effortless, a wonderful coarse gesture.

Swap "cards" for "pages," and you get the web's longstanding metaphor. But even the first generations of touchscreen browsers forced you to flip through these pages by tapping a button, confusing the metaphor. When was the last time you turned a paper page by hitting a button? Most touchscreen browsers now do the right thing, letting you swipe through page history. After decades of using a physical metaphor—the page—to describe the web, we've finally arrived at a physical interaction to match.

This reconciliation is the crucial work of touchscreen interaction design. Embrace the verbs that obviously match your interface's nouns. Consider everything you can do to a card in the real world: flip, fold, shuffle, stack, turn over, stretch, sort, crumple, dog-ear, throw aside. All those physical actions are available as a springboard for your interface metaphor. What does it mean to flip over a data object, to stretch it, to crumple it?

Facebook created an app called Paper to play on this card-like physicality, revealing a uniquely touch-friendly way to explore the Facebook timeline. Everything is represented as a card. The app is organized into feeds, represented as decks that you can sort, shuffle, or discard to create new collections. Each item in a feed is a card that you can flip through. When a card features a web article, you swipe up to unfold it like a newspaper and start reading (**FIG 4.9**).

The gestures in Facebook Paper have a natural logic once discovered, but they're not always obvious to the newcomer. Helping your audience find, learn, and adapt to these new gestures is a major challenge—one we'll tackle in the next chapter.

That said, when gestures hinge on simple interactions based on the physical world, you may not have to do much education. As we embark on designing interactions beyond the basics, let's begin by looking around us for inspiration.

To make sense of the world, we put our trust in a mix of physical laws and human conventions. Gravity has proven to be awfully reliable, for one, and so have many of our own social constructions (salt and pepper shakers notwithstanding). Screws turn clockwise, the pages of Western books proceed from left to right, a checkmark signifies a completed task, and red means stop. These things set our expectations and shape our behaviors as we move through the physical world. Apply those expectations and behaviors to your touchscreen interface, and you give your users a familiar and predictable experience. Here are a few strategies to do so.

Borrow one-to-one interactions

The most no-nonsense approach is to interact with the screen exactly as we interact with another real-world object. Sketchpads are a straightforward example, creating the illusion (again!) that the touchscreen is interchangeable with a piece of paper (there's a reason we call these things pads and tablets). Take Paper (an iPad drawing app not to be confused with Facebook Paper), which has gone to remarkable technical lengths to recreate ink on paper. Choose among pencils, pens, or nibs and draw with a stylus or your finger. Freeform painting becomes the app's primary gestural interaction—the same action that works in the real world also works on the tablet—simple.

Often, though, you can borrow a familiar physical interaction without copying the entire original artifact. You know how a knob or dial works: cranking clockwise means more or forward; counter-clockwise means less or backward. But if you want to use that *crank* motion, you don't have to add an actual knob to your interface. Instead, use the action as inspiration for

---

FIG 4.10: Want to undo? Crank to rewind in Paper.

a gestural equivalent. The Paper app does this well: cranking two fingers counter-clockwise anywhere onscreen performs the undo action, traveling back in time to remove strokes from your drawing. Change your mind? Crank clockwise to redraw your strokes (FIG 4.10). As you borrow from the real world, remember that it's the physical *action* you seek to import, not the original object; it's about the crank, not the knob.

Lean on established symbols or notation

As we translate physical cranking motions to screen gesture, we transform them into *notations,* a meaningful shorthand. These symbols are human inventions—clockwise and counter-clockwise doodles have no inherent meaning in nature. But again, all user interface is social construction; lifting from

Proofreaders' Marks

OPERATIONAL SIGNS

Delete

Close up; delete space

Delete and close up (use only when deleting letters *within* a word)

Let it stand

Insert space

Make space between words equal; make space between lines equal

Insert hair space

Letterspace

Begin new paragraph

Indent type one em from left or right

Move right

Move left

Center

Move up

Move down

Flush left

Flush right

Straighten type; align horizontally

Align vertically

Transpose

Spell out

TYPOGRAPHICAL SIGNS

Set in italic type

Set in roman type

Set in boldface type

Set in lowercase

Set in capital letters

Set in small capitals

Wrong font; set in correct type

Check type image; remove blemish

Insert here *or* make superscript

Insert here *or* make subscript

PUNCTUATION MARKS

Insert comma

Insert apostrophe *or* single quotation mark

Insert quotation marks

Insert period

Insert question mark

Insert semicolon

Insert colon

Insert hyphen

Insert em dash

Insert en dash

Insert parentheses

FIG 4.11: *The Chicago Manual of Style*'s collection of proofreaders' marks (http://bkaprt.com/dft/04-03/).

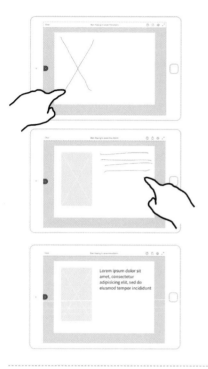

FIG 4.12: Adobe Comp borrows the sketch notation of wireframing. Here, drawing an X adds an image placeholder, and tracing a series of lines inserts text.

well-known conventions makes your interface feel instantly familiar, intuitive.

Sometimes entire notation systems can be borrowed whole cloth. The specialized set of proofreaders' marks, for example, is at once expressive of complex ideas and universally understood among editors (FIG 4.11). An application aimed at that audience might adapt that notation into shorthand gestures to delete, move, or insert new paragraphs.

Adobe Comp is a wireframing app for iPad, and its touch-friendly interface piggybacks on common wireframe symbols (FIG 4.12). Add an image by tracing a big X, drop in a column of text by scrawling a stack of lines, erase an element by scribbling it out. The app converts these symbols into wireframe components and, when you're done, exports to InDesign, Illustrator, or Photoshop—casual whiteboard-style input transformed into formal wireframe output. Now, this may not be any more efficient than producing a wireframe with Microsoft Visio or OmniGraffle on a desktop, but it's the quickest way to do it on a touchscreen. These fluid, sketch-like gestures create layouts much faster than a marathon of taps through a series of desktop-style control panels.

Apply physics to digital objects

Adobe Comp borrows directly from how we work a familiar interface—paper—but you don't have to be so literal. You can also apply real-world physics to digital objects by giving them a sense of mass, of physical presence. For instance, pinch-to-zoom lends squeeze-n-stretch physicality to photos or maps. The way a scrolling screen bounces when you slam into the end of content adds solidity to intangible data. The iPhone app Clear treats to-do-list items like physical building blocks that you can squeeze, slide, or nudge aside, and those actions have semantic meaning for the data (**FIG 4.13**):

- Insert a new list item by spreading your fingers between two other items to make room.
- Mark an item complete by pushing it aside with a swipe.
- Pinch a list to close it.

These are simple gestures for simple physical actions, mapping naturally to how you might rearrange list items if they were arranged physically on your desk. When virtual elements behave with such familiar physicality, our brains flow naturally into the interaction.

Honor physical constraints

If things we can do in the physical world inspire gestural interactions, so too do things we *can't*. TouchUp is an iPad app that draws filters or effects on photos. The simplest example is painting a color on the photo, using your finger as a brush. But what if you want to change the brush size? That's easy, right? After all, desktop apps always address this by offering either a slider or a brush palette to choose a new brush size. Thing is,

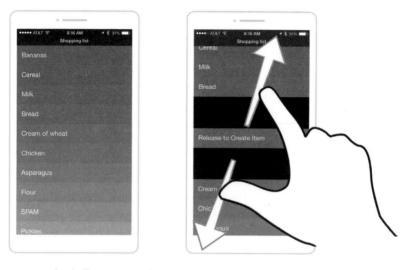

FIG 4.13: Clear's all-gesture interface relies on simple physicality. To insert a list item, spread two items apart to make room.

you already have a brush—your finger—*and it doesn't change size.* Changing the size of your finger's impression on the screen to anything other than the size of your fingertip introduces uncertainty. You have no idea how large a mark you'll leave. You shift from direct interaction to abstract guesswork.

So TouchUp doesn't let you change brush size. Instead, you change the canvas size: pinch to zoom out and spread to zoom in. Your finger brush is always the same size onscreen, but because you're drawing on a super-zoomed photo, the result is a fine line on the image.

It seems obvious when you see it in action, but it turns the traditional desktop approach on its head. When you deal with the physicality of touch, you have to rethink familiar solutions. With every solution, ask yourself: does the old way still make sense, or does direct interaction demand a new approach?

When you use the real world as your guide, you create interfaces that are instantly understandable. Some actions, however, are freighted with more meaning or complexity than can be easily packed into a simple physical action; they may require more abstract gestures. Those advanced power moves have a parallel in traditional computing.

GESTURES AS THE KEYBOARD SHORTCUTS OF TOUCH

Quick-to-discover gestures, combined with well-labeled traditional controls, should always form the foundation of your interface. Always make it easy to figure out your application's basic actions. But don't shy from deploying more abstract gesture shortcuts as *alternatives* alongside standard controls, like keyboard shortcuts on the desktop. Earlier, for example, I mentioned that the iPad Mail app supplements the back button with a coarse swipe. Or, from Chapter 3, take Vimeo, where a gesture inside a list view saves a trip to the detail page: swipe left or right across a video to share or favorite it. In both cases, the "slow way" is still available, but gestures are expert power moves.

These speedy shortcuts aren't restricted to swipes and taps. More fingers multiply the possibilities. A five-finger touch might toggle between views of Sent mail and the Inbox. In a newspaper app, a two-finger swipe could fast-forward to the next section, not just the next page. A future of multifinger gestures promises a richer interaction language, where abstract gestures help shoulder complex actions.

The unrealized potential of multifinger gestures

The iPad app Uzu is "a kinetic particle visualizer," but your first impression of it might be more like a toy to hypnotize stoners, an interactive lava lamp. Touch the screen with one finger and sparks shoot off like fireworks (**FIG 4.14**). Add a second, and sparks swirl between the two, while a third finger creates a vortex among all three. Change the hue and particle size by touching the screen with all ten fingers and swiping up and down, or left and right. As you get the hang of it, your fingers fly and dance across the screen, and it feels like playing a kind of technicolor visual keyboard—more instrument than tool.

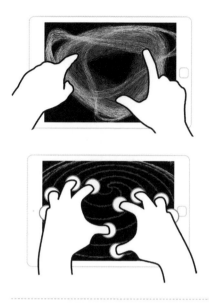

FIG 4.14: In Uzu, different finger counts trigger different animations and actions.

At first blush, this might not seem relevant to that financial services intranet app that you have to build, but Uzu offers useful lessons for all kinds of touch interfaces. In particular, this multifinger approach recalls the role of Alt, Command, or Function keys; ten fingers afford ten modes or actions. *Fingers become function keys.* Just as expert typists fly through words, or power users deploy keyboard shortcuts to fly through tasks, multitouch gestures likewise help us to move effortlessly through touch interfaces. These gestures, while abstract, allow power users to accomplish tasks more economically.

If multifinger commands possess such powerful potential, why don't we have more of them? While phones have supported multitouch for years, they're not great at it. One-handed grips and small screens have encouraged us to tap away with a single finger or thumb instead. Larger screens hold more promise. The size and weight of larger tablets requires you to use two hands or rest the tablet on your lap, so you always have at least one hand free—with a screen big enough to invite multiple touches at once. The same goes for hybrids and laptops.

Obstacles exist, though. Accessibility is a major one: not everyone has full mobility of hands and fingers—or even all their fingers, for that matter. For certain disabilities, a five-finger pinch is a non-starter. Discoverability is another stumbling block. How are we supposed to know when abstract actions like a three-finger swipe or a five-finger touch are even available? We'll turn to strategies for revealing gestures in Chapter 5, but consider it best to treat these more abstract multitouch gestures as alternatives—expressive supplements to buttons and other traditional interactions. People should still be able to accomplish any action with simple taps and swipes, though it may take longer.

NAVIGATING HEAVY GESTURE TRAFFIC

As you layer more and more gestures into your interface to supplement or replace traditional controls, those gestures start to get crowded. For one, the operating systems and browsers claim key gestures so that your app or website has to scrabble among the leftovers; for another, gestures—especially coarse gestures—eat up lots of room and jostle for space on the screen.

Make way for system and browser gestures

As a designer, you have to jockey with browsers and operating systems for key gestures—and if the system gets there first, it wins. Remember Android's screen-bottom system buttons in Chapter 1? The operating system has first claim, so app designers must make way, taking their controls to the top of the screen. The same goes for system gestures; app designers have to work around the operating environment to avoid gesture conflicts.

iOS for iPad, for example, offers coarse gestures to move between apps. Swipe left or right with four or five fingers to switch among recent apps, or pinch with four or five fingers to close an app and zip out to the home screen. You can just slap at the whole screen to navigate apps—exactly the kind of coarse gestures that a tablet OS should embrace. I'm a huge fan of the spirit of these gestures, but I'm not wild on the execution. If only Apple had followed the interaction already adopted by other platforms, like Windows and more than a few defunct touch operating systems, including Symbian, BlackBerry Play-Book, and Palm's WebOS. They all use *edge gestures,* a technique that is both more internally consistent and more deferential to individual apps. Edge gestures start on the frame, or bezel, of the device and swipe into the canvas. When used for app switching, this creates the illusion of knocking screens aside by shoving them at the edge.

Edge gestures match physical action with the conceptual metaphor of the OS. If you consider apps as the front-and-center canvas of the device, then the operating system is the frame that supports that canvas. When OS-level gestures start from the bezel, action matches expectation: this gesture works outside the current app. You're working on the frame—the operating system—both physically and metaphorically.

In contrast, iPad's app-switching actions work within the canvas itself, territory that should be dedicated to the current app. This creates confusing competition with app interaction: Will this gesture apply at the app level or at the operating-system level? Apple could have avoided this ambiguity by anchoring its gestures at the edge. By putting them inside the canvas, Apple swiped some great gestures from designers' arsenals.

Browsers also claim a hefty share of useful gestures for themselves. Pinch, double-tap, swipe, long-press... These core gestures already have meaning in browsers, taking them off the table for web designers. You *could* override those gestures by capturing their touch events and hijacking them for your own purposes—to make a long press trigger a custom behavior instead of showing a contextual menu, for example. But breaking a browser feature is almost never a good idea. Making browser gestures work inconsistently across websites undermines user confidence when we still need to shore up gestural interactions and establish standards. Let browsers have their gestures and work with what's left.

Give your gestures elbow room

Managing gesture density means more than avoiding browser and OS conflicts; you also need to consider the physical space these gestures occupy, or they begin to overlap and collide. When gestures pile up, so do user errors. Consider a photo gallery that lets you swipe back and forth through photos inside a single web page. On small screens, these swipes easily run afoul of browsers' edge gestures; mobile Safari, for example, reserves edge-swiping left or right to cruise through your browser history. In our photo hypothetical, a wide accidental swipe while browsing the gallery would jump you out of the experience entirely, dumping you into another page from your history. Previous versions of Chrome for Android sidestepped this problem by limiting gesture real estate. A left or right swipe from the edge used to change tabs, but people kept switching them by accident while swiping within the page. So Chrome's developers limited the tab-hopping gesture to a swipe across the address bar, instead of anywhere on the page. The move gave space and freedom to gesture-wielding web designers. (Chrome finally gave up on tabs altogether in Android 5.0 Lollipop.)

Ease risky gesture density by anticipating it. That swiping gallery might use the HTML5 history API to update the browser history with each swipe. An accidental edge swipe backward in that scenario would return you to the previous slide—the same result as a regular swipe in the gallery.

Radial menus reduce gesture density

Sometimes old techniques resurface to solve new problems. The radial menu rolled out half a century ago but may have finally found its moment as a way to sidestep gesture conflicts. A radial menu is a set of options that spin out like spokes from a wheel. Microsoft's note-taking app OneNote, for example, features a radial menu as a kind of right-click contextual menu (FIG 4.15). Tap the app's ever-present menu icon, and out pops a wheel of actions to apply to your current selection. Drag your finger to the one you want and release.

FIG 4.15: OneNote's radial contextual menu.

At first glance, these menus might seem more complicated than a plain toolbar, full of visual information to process. At their core, though, radial menus are gesture-based: touch-swipe-release. That's why some call radial menus "marking menus": it's like making a mark on the screen. Swiping to two o'clock has one meaning, and swiping to six o'clock another. You get faster over time, because radial menus take advantage of muscle memory in a way that list-based menus cannot. In iOS Messages, for instance, you trigger radial menus to text an audio clip, photo, or video (**FIG 4.16**). It's a fluid motion that quickly becomes a habit.

Another benefit is that radial menus keep their gestures very compact. They start from a specific point on the screen—ideally on the content that you seek to manipulate, though often on a menu button or other trigger instead. This fixed anchor point reduces errors by demanding extra care; it asks you to press on the element you want to affect before launching into the gesture. Radial menus are more precise and help bring order to otherwise crowded gesture interfaces.

Radial menus have been around since the late 1960s but until recently never got much traction in traditional mainstream interfaces, with one exception: games. Combat-based games use radial menus for speedy access to inventory or combat options (**FIG 4.17**). It makes good sense that trigger-finger games have adopted the radial menu over a more typical list. In games,

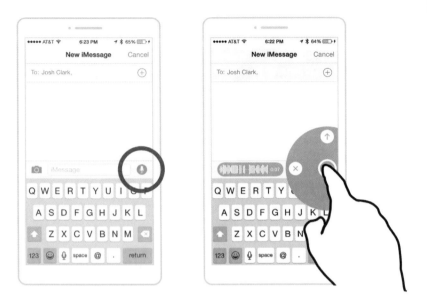

FIG 4.16: Tap and hold the microphone icon, and a radial menu pops up as the app starts recording: flick up to send the audio; flick left to delete; or let go to pause.

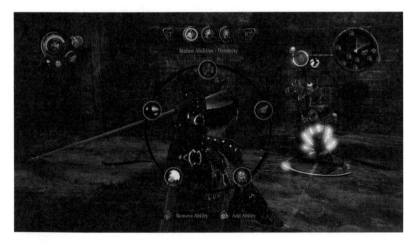

FIG 4.17: The kind-of-awesomely-named *Game of Thrones: The Game* uses a radial menu to control the action.

limiting interruptions is essential to the experience, and radial menus are more efficient than other selection tools.

The research on this has been in the can for over twenty-five years. A 1988 study did the comparison and found that for a specific test of eight-item lists, users were faster with radial menus than linear lists (http://bkaprt.com/dft/04-04/). And it turns out that speed only improves. That was borne out in a 1994 study by Bill Buxton and Gordon Kurtenbach, who tested radial-menu speed with a stylus. Over time, they found that expert users stopped looking at the menu at all, marking the screen with no-look gestures instead of pecking at buttons. Once they made that transition, selection became three times faster (http://bkaprt.com/dft/04-05/).

Like any technique, however, radial menus have their limitations too. Keep in mind the following caveats:

- **They demand precision.** While a radial menu's fixed anchor point reduces gesture density, this is also at odds with the benefits of screen-roaming coarse gestures. Coarse gestures are ideal for navigation and basic controls, while radial menus are better suited for quick actions and tools.
- **They don't scale.** You can only cram so many items around a circle. Eight seems to be the reasonable maximum. On smaller screens like phones, a radial menu gobbles up an especially big share of pixels, so it's typically limited to three or four options.
- **First use might be awkward.** Despite the speed boost that comes with experience, we're more at ease scanning down a list than around a circle. But that comfort level may not be so important when you look at actual use. "The effects of organization disappear with practice," Buxton found in 1994. "Even when menu items have a natural linear ordering, selection using a radial menu is still faster and less error-prone than selection using a linear menu." This fact, however, relies on rolling with one last constraint:
- **Radial menus must be consistent.** If you change the order or content of a radial menu dynamically, people fall back to visual selection, and you lose out on the muscle-memory speed boost.

FIG 4.18: The iPhone apps for Yelp (left) and My Fitness Pal (right) use radial menus in their navigation.

On the whole, these limitations are modest—and actually help shape good use cases for radial menus, like primary navigation or consistent contextual menus. That's exactly the role they've come to play in parts of Android, Windows, and iOS, as well as menu navigation for many popular apps (FIG 4.18).

Radial menus have been slower to arrive on the web than those system and app environments, even though they're well suited to both the medium and browser capabilities. Existing web examples include the occasional jQuery plugin (http://bkaprt.com/dft/04-06/) or a CSS3 clone of the Path app's radial menu (http://bkaprt.com/dft/04-07/). Why aren't we seeing more of these experiments? Truth is, it's still painful to develop gestures in the browser. Let's look at why.

THE HEARTACHE OF GESTURES ON THE WEB

Some structural problems make designing browser-based gestures vexing, though not impossible. Browsers aren't yet very good at meeting the interaction expectations that touchscreen devices have created, thanks to a couple of reasons in particular.

First, as we saw earlier, browsers already claim so many useful gestures for themselves. These gesture conflicts leave little to the designer beyond tap and swipe. (This is also why radial menus are a good fit for the web: their tap-swipe interaction neatly uses the available combo.)

Second, JavaScript gives front-end developers only the most basic touch events: `touchstart`, `touchend`, and `touchmove`. It's easy enough to detect a tap or maybe a swipe, but anything trickier gets complicated fast. Have fun coding a crank gesture, a two-finger rotation, or a multifinger swipe. Ideally, we'd have events for common gestures on any DOM element: pinch, long tap, swipe, rotate, and more. (Microsoft models this in its framework for building native Windows apps with HTML5, perhaps suggesting a way forward.) For now, we have to build them ourselves from scratch—or better, use a library like the excellent Hammer.js (http://hammerjs.github.io), which provides events for tap, double-tap, swipe, drag, pinch, and rotate.

Tools and techniques are emerging to help designers cope. Swipes are a particularly good place to start. They're (relatively) easy to implement, and many sites already embrace swipe for next/previous navigation. For instance, you can swipe through Flickr's photo galleries, next/previous articles at the *New York Times,* Google's image search, and lots more.

You can venture beyond swipe, of course, but it's harder work. Let's examine what's involved. The rest of this chapter introduces how browsers wrangle touch events and how you can use JavaScript and/or CSS to construct a few simple gestures. While we won't sink into the gritty details—this isn't a JavaScript tome—it's important for designers to understand what's realistic when coding for touch. Because coding touch events is never trivial, let's start with when you *don't* need them.

STICK WITH CLICK

As noted, most touchscreen browsers offer `touchstart`, `touchmove`, and `touchend` events. Tapping the screen also triggers good old-fashioned `click`, which allows swaths of mouse-focused code in legacy sites to get their jobs done in a touch environment. You can salvage your sanity by focusing on that single interaction model.

Whenever possible, stick with click. Despite the availability of more complex touch events, you don't need to replace click events in your JavaScript unless you're after something fancier than a tap. While we colloquially associate click with the mouse, it's not strictly a mouse event. Instead, consider it a generic action: "I want to activate this element." In most cases, if you want to trigger something when a user taps, capturing click does the trick. Skip the touch events and proceed as if you were coding for mouse.

Sticking with click has the added benefit of working across inputs. Despite its mouse-derived name, click is likely to remain the key action for web browsers whether they're driven by keyboard, speech, Kinect-style air gesture, or perhaps even a virtual-reality head twitch. *Click is not only backward compatible; it's future compatible too.*

But click isn't perfect. Much of this chapter has made the case that touch demands new approaches. Touch interactions vary in ways both obvious and subtle from mouse or trackpad events. Not least is the number of pointers to contend with. Mouse interfaces never have more than one cursor clicking away; with touch, you get the possibility of ten fingers (or even more with the help of friends—or toes). If you need to track more than one finger at once, click won't cut it. Use click when you can, but switch to touch events when you need to do any of these:

- Track multiple touches (pinch, rotate, or two-finger swipe)
- Take action while the finger is pressed to the screen (a touch-flavored mouseover)
- Track finger motion (a swipe or drag)

On this last item, you sometimes get some wiggle room. No-frills CSS has you covered for the most common swiping use case—galleries and carousels—so let's begin there.

USE CSS FOR GALLERY AND
CAROUSEL SWIPING

Sites often rely on complex JavaScript to create carousels and their associated swipes, but that overengineers a surprisingly simple solution. If you instead use overflow:scroll in CSS, all modern touchscreen browsers will give you hardware-accelerated panning; swiping comes for free, no JavaScript required.

Consider a list of images:

```
<ul class="carousel">
  <li>
      <img src="image1.png" alt="unicorn">
  </li>
  <li>
      <img src="image2.png" alt="rainbow">
  </li>
  <li>
      <img src="image3.png" alt="sparkles">
  </li>
</ul>
```

Use CSS to display the list items inline in a horizontal strip, all set to a specific size:

```
.carousel {
  white-space:nowrap;
}
.carousel li {
  display: inline-block;
  padding: 0;
  margin: 0;
}
.carousel img {
  width: 400px;
  height: 300px;
}
```

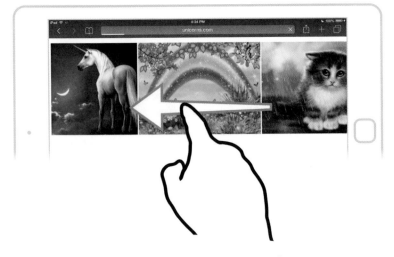

FIG 4.19: Who needs JavaScript? CSS and HTML are all you need to create a swiping carousel.

And here's the magic. Set the height and width of the containing ul list, and set its horizontal overflow (overflow-x) to scroll. This tells browsers to scroll the images when they can't all fit the available width. The result: touchscreen browsers display a horizontally swipeable carousel of images (**FIG 4.19**).

```
.carousel {
    white-space:nowrap;
    overflow-x: scroll;
    overflow-y: hidden;
    width: 100%;
    height: 300px;

    /* add momentum scrolling for mobile Safari */
    -webkit-overflow-scrolling: touch;
}
```

The last rule of the `.carousel` styles tells iOS to apply fancy *momentum scrolling:*

```
-webkit-overflow-scrolling: touch;
```

Now, a flick of the finger sends the page scrolling and it continues under its own momentum, easing to a stop for an effect that mimics natural physical behavior. Without `-webkit-overflow-scrolling`, the carousel would move only when you dragged it, with a hard stop, for a clunky, artificial interaction. Other modern touch browsers don't need this hint and include momentum scrolling with no extra help.

A caveat: many older mobile browsers don't handle `overflow:scroll` properly and instead treat it like `overflow:hidden`, which lops off any content that doesn't fit. Instead of a zippy carousel, you're left with one that won't budge, putting any overflow out of reach. Happily, Filament Group has a fix: Overthrow is a JavaScript library that nudges these browsers to do the right thing, and throws in momentum scrolling to boot (http://bkaprt.com/dft/04-08/).

Add snap points to the carousel

We now have a free-spinning carousel, which is great except that it can come to rest midway between images. Make the carousel snap to one of its panels when it stops scrolling by adding `scroll-snap` rules:

```css
.carousel {
    white-space:nowrap;
    overflow-x: scroll;
    overflow-y: hidden;
    width: 100%;
    height: 300px;

    /* add momentum scrolling for mobile Safari */
    -webkit-overflow-scrolling: touch;
```

```
/* snap to panels when it stops scrolling */
-ms-scroll-snap-type: mandatory;
scroll-snap-type: mandatory;
-ms-scroll-snap-points-x: snapInterval(0px,
400px);
scroll-snap-points-x: snapInterval(0px, 400px);
}
```

The scroll-snap-points-x rule tells the carousel to snap at the start of the first image (at 0px of the carousel's width) and then snap to every 400px from there, the width of every following image. At this writing, only Internet Explorer 10+ supports scroll-snap, and other browsers ignore it, scrolling fast and free without snapping. scroll-snap is on the standards track, however, so more browsers may adopt it in the future (http://bkaprt.com/dft/04-09/).

Tidy the desktop experience with progressive enhancement

On mobile and tablet browsers, elements with overflow:scroll are visually uncluttered. On desktop, though, these elements sprout scroll bars. Scroll bars are a fine starting point; they allow people to access your content, with a clear visual cue that more content is available. But oy, scroll bars on mid-page carousels sure make for clunky visuals. Apply some carefully crafted JavaScript to enhance the experience. Use JavaScript to detect if the browser has touch or pointer objects and, if not, set the carousel to overflow:hidden and add next/previous buttons to move the .carousel contents left and right. I leave the details of coding this desktop carousel as an exercise for the reader, but first, a few notes. As we discussed in Chapter 1, detecting touch is not foolproof. For this specific widget, though, this is enough for a strictly aesthetic upgrade:

```
if ( ! 'ontouchstart' in window ||
     ! window.navigator.MaxTouchPoints ||
     ! window.navigator.msMaxTouchPoints )
{
```

```
// no touch, build next/previous buttons for
desktop
}
```

Because this touch detection isn't airtight, this approach will inevitably give some touch browsers the next/previous buttons instead of swiping. Don't fret. It will be a small minority of browsers, your content will still be accessible, and with chunky next/previous buttons, it will stay touch-friendly.

TOUCH EVENTS IN THE BROWSER

As you've seen, a savvy mix of CSS and JavaScript `click` events can handle tap and swipe. If that's all you need, our work is done; feel free to hop over to the next chapter. But if you need more complex gestures—multitouch, drag and drop, crank, rotate, and so on—it's time to buckle up, put on your crash helmet, and code touch events. We won't go far down the coding rabbit hole, but here's a high-level overview of how touch events work.

The iPhone was the first popular platform to build JavaScript touch events into the browser, and other browser vendors quickly followed suit to provide compatibility with iOS. This approach became a W3C standard (http://bkaprt.com/dft/04-10/), and it's now supported by nearly all modern touch browsers (except Internet Explorer, which has its own competing pointer model that may itself become a separate standard. We'll look at that in a moment).

The prevailing touch-event model lets developers detect three events: `touchstart`, `touchend`, and `touchmove`. You may be familiar with their desktop cousins `mousedown`, `mouseup`, and `mousemove`, and these touch events work similarly: developers can detect when a touch begins, ends, or changes, and then trigger corresponding actions on the page. These events, like all JavaScript events, create an *event data object* that developers can access to get more information about the touch. Touch-event objects include three lists of *touches,* data objects that each refer to a finger or stylus currently touching the screen:

- `event.touches`: a list of *all* touch objects on the screen, not just the DOM element for this event
- `event.targetTouches`: a focused list of touch objects that includes only the touches on the current DOM element
- `event.changedTouches`: a list of the touch objects involved in the current event. In `touchmove`, for example, this list tells you which touches actually moved. Say that you're pinching with your finger and thumb, but only your thumb moves. Then only that touch would be included here.

Each of the touch objects in these three lists in turn contains information about the coordinates of the touch and the target element that triggered the event. (If you touch a link, for example, the target element is that link's `<a>` DOM element.) These event and touch objects enable developers to track the presence, position, and motion of fingers on the screen. For an introduction, check out the tutorial by Boris Smus, "Developing for Multi-Touch Web Browsers" (http://bkaprt.com/dft/04-11/).

Untangling mouse and touch events

Earlier we covered how touch triggers a `click` event for backward compatibility, but that touch triggers a whole range of other mouse events too. Every time you touch and lift your finger to the screen, the browser fires off all of these events, in this order: `touchstart`, `touchmove` (if applicable), `touchend`, `mouseover`, `mousemove` (if applicable), `mousedown`, `mouseup`, `click`. This behavior is intended to make sure that sites coded for mouse-and-cursor interaction will continue to work on touchscreens, which is a good thing. However, a few tricky elements are worth calling out:

- Mouse events all happen in a flurry *after* the finger lifts off the screen. So `touchmove` doesn't happen at the same time as `mousemove`, and `mouseover` is triggered when the finger isn't even on the screen anymore. While mouse events remain available, in other words, they don't match touch behavior one to one.

- Because a touch triggers both touch and mouse events, take care when defining separate actions on both mouse *and* touch events so that you don't double up. Use `event.preventDefault()` inside touch event handlers to keep the browser from firing the corresponding mouse events, too. (This has some repercussions, which we'll discuss.) For example, if you want to do something on `touchstart` for touch and `mousedown` for mouse, you need to tell the browser not to process any other touch events when `touchstart` is triggered or it will do the `mousedown` action too:

```
document.body.addEventListener('touchstart',
  function(event) {
  event.preventDefault(); // don't trigger more
  events for this touch

  // your code for the touchstart event goes here
}, false);
```

- There's a 300-millisecond delay after `touchend`, so `click` and all other simulated mouse events fire a full third of a second after you lift your finger off the screen. (This also means that only one `mousemove` event occurs for any given touch, while `touchmove` updates as you move your finger.) We'll see why this delay happens and how you can eliminate it in a bit.
- You lose the semantic meaning of mouse events like `mouseout`, which is triggered on the touched element only after *another* page element is touched, not when you lift your finger, as you might expect.

In many cases, the differences between touch and mouse dictate that you work out separate interaction styles for each, supporting each input independently. To magnify an element, for example, you might add pinch and spread detection for touch events while switching to button-driven zooming for mouse events. But it gets more complicated when you consider the growing number of devices and browsers that let you switch back and forth between mouse, keyboard, and touch.

Your interface must be prepared to accept any available style of input and interaction. If you're a JavaScript developer, get used to writing separate code for clicks and for touches, which fast becomes a heavy burden.

The responsibility of taking over touch events

As mentioned above, you have to use `preventDefault()` in touch event handlers to stop the browser from triggering corresponding mouse events too. Simple enough, but it has a major side effect: in addition to canceling mouse events for that touch, it tells the browser not to follow any of its usual default behavior on the element—no scrolling, no clicks, and so on. When you trap a touch event with `preventDefault()`, you effectively tell the browser that you'll take it from here and handle *everything* related to that touch. Is the user trying to tap, scroll, swipe, double-tap? You have to sort that out and provide that behavior yourself. For example, when you use `preventDefault()` in a `touchstart` or `touchmove` event handler, you cancel scrolling for that touch. Either you code your own scrolling behavior or that part of the page becomes a no-scroll zone.

Handling low-level interactions like this gets complicated in a hurry, and you don't want to plunge down this path lightly. If you do start the trek (and you have to if you want any kind of complex gesture), consider limiting your custom `touchend` handlers to a small number of buttons or links. In particular, avoid adding touch handlers to scrolling elements so that you don't inadvertently disable the browser's usual scrolling behavior.

Again, if you can make do with the `click` event, you'll save yourself one hundred kinds of pain. Unfortunately, even our reliable friend `click` has its eccentricities when it comes to touch. Topmost is the noticeable delay between when you touch the screen and when a touch is triggered.

MANAGING THE 300-MILLISECOND DELAY

Until very recently, every touch-based mobile browser imposed a 300 ms delay before registering a "click" after you tapped the screen. That's a third of a second, enough to make touchscreen websites feel sluggish compared to apps. The culprit is the double-tap gesture touch browsers use for zooming in and out of a page. When you tap the screen once, the browser waits a few beats—300 ms!—to respond, to ensure you're not in the middle of a double-tap. If it weren't for that one-two tap, browsers could proceed without delay.

Most browsers reserve the double-tap for zooming only, so Chrome and Firefox for Android try something crafty: they won't wait for a double-tap if the designer disables zooming on the page from the get-go. Problem is, preventing page zoom nixes not only double-tap but also pinch-to-zoom, a function many need to be able to read your site. For them, disabling zoom effectively breaks your site—a crummy thing to do for accessibility.

In 2013, Chrome took a more useful step, throwing out double-tap zooming when a page fixes its width to device-width, like so:

```
<meta name="viewport" content="width=device-width,
   initial-scale=1.0">
```

If you're designing a responsive or mobile-only site, you should be using that tag anyway, so it's an easy win that skips the 300 ms delay without extra effort. Bonus: pinch zooming remains available. Other browsers may eventually follow Chrome's example, but some cannot. Mobile Safari, for instance, scrolls the page when you double-tap at the top or bottom of the screen. It's unlikely to disable the gesture anytime soon, as the double-tap does more than zoom.

Internet Explorer lets you turn off double-tap zooming with CSS. Using the touch-action property (http://bkaprt.com/dft/04-12/), you can tell IE 10+ whether to permit default touch behavior on individual elements. For example, to disable double-taps on an element while still allowing pinches, add this CSS rule:

```
-ms-touch-action: manipulation;
touch-action: manipulation;
```

It's a cinch. To sum up, get fast, no-wait taps in Chrome and Internet Explorer like so:

- Set the viewport to `device-width`.
- Use the `touch-action` CSS rule.

Other browsers will still slouch along with a delay, but if you really need to speed things up, a pair of JavaScript libraries can help. FastClick by FT Labs (http://bkaprt.com/dft/04-13/) uses touch events to trigger fast clicks, and it removes the double-tap gesture. It also takes on the hard work of differentiating scrolls, swipes, and taps for you. Tappy by Filament Group's Scott Jehl (http://bkaprt.com/dft/04-14/) papers over the differences among touch, mouse, and keyboard `click` events by creating a single `tap` event that works for all three, eliminating the 300 ms delay in the process.

THE PAIN AND PROMISE OF POINTER EVENTS

So here I am, suggesting a JavaScript library to unify clicks and touches as one event. Or telling you to use `click` wherever possible. I've been dancing around it, but oh careful reader, you've no doubt detected an earnest desire for a single codebase that works for both mouse and touch—at least for straightforward interactions. Different inputs will always demand different interactions, so separate code is sometimes necessary. But for the basics (clicks, scrolling, drag and drop, etc.) the interactions are so similar, we shouldn't have to treat them separately. That's the idea behind *pointer events*.

Microsoft introduced pointer events in Internet Explorer 10 as a competing alternative to touch events. Pointer events merge events for mouse, touch, and stylus, and possibly even things like Kinect-style air gestures—anything that points. They show promise, but unfortunately, they work only in Internet Explorer. That may change; the W3C has created a pointer-events standard (http://bkaprt.com/dft/04-15/), which other browsers might adopt (at this writing, Chrome and Firefox say they will, and Safari says it won't). While this browser intrigue plays out, JavaScript libraries like Hand.js from Microsoft (http://bkaprt.com/dft/04-16/) fill the gap and let you use pointer events immediately for unified event handling in all browsers. In any case, designers are obliged to support touch events *and* pointer events *and* mouse events. Oof. Here's a quick review of how the pointer system works. Pointers trigger varied events and, unlike mouse actions, they can happen simultaneously (e.g., when you touch several fingers to the screen). For compatibility, mouse events still get called, so as with touch events, make sure you don't process both pointer and mouse events—event.preventDefault() is your friend, with the caveats mentioned earlier.

Because Microsoft released Internet Explorer 10 ahead of the W3C's standard, the company used vendor prefixes to name their own pointer events. Now that the standard's complete, these prefixed names are no longer supported, starting in IE 11. In other words, to cover all versions, you need to attach both the prefixed and non-prefixed names of pointer events and objects. It gets wordy. The key pointer events are:

- pointerdown (or MSPointerDown for IE 10): a mouse button is pressed, or a finger or stylus makes contact with the screen. Similar to mousedown and touchstart.
- pointerup (or MSPointerUp): a mouse button is released, or a finger or stylus is lifted. Similar to mouseup and touchend.
- pointermove (or MSPointerMove): an active pointer is in motion. Similar to mousemove and touchmove.
- pointerover (or MSPointerOver): start of hover; for devices that don't support hover, this event is fired immediately before pointerdown. Similar to mouseover.
- pointerout (or MSPointerOut); end of hover; for non-hovering gadgets, this event is fired immediately after pointerup. Similar to mouseout.

The pointer-event object gives you all the information that a mouse event would (event.clientX and event.clientY for screen coordinates, event.target for the target element, etc.) But the object also reveals the kind of pointer you received (event.pointerType) or even how much pressure a stylus is exerting (`event.pressure`). For full details about working with pointer-event objects, check out Microsoft's Pointer Events documentation (http://bkaprt.com/dft/04-17/).

All together now: supporting pointer, touch, and click

Whew, now we're juggling a jackpot of event types: keyboard, mouse, touch, pointer, and Microsoft's prefixed pointer names. How do you wrangle your JavaScript? First set up pointer events for browsers that support them and, for the rest, set up mouse and touch events separately. Then give all browsers keyboard and `click` events. Here's the rundown:

```
if ('PointerEvent' in window) {
  // bind to pointer events
}
else if ('MSPointerEvent' in window) {
  // bind to MS-prefixed pointer events
}
else {
  // bind to mouse events

  if ('ontouchstart' in window) {
    // bind to touch events;
    // use event.preventDefault() to avoid
  processing both touch
    // and mouse events
  }
}
// bind to keyboard events
// bind to click events
```

Pointer events have terrific potential to gather interaction events under one umbrella, but in the interim, they add yet another scenario for designers to manage—along with the associated code bloat and performance cost of including this extra code. Your best tack? Simplify where you can and lean on the common `click` event (or `tap` from the Tappy library).

Touchscreens create interaction expectations that browsers aren't yet adept at. For better or worse—simple or complex—this is how we build gestures on the web. Because the touch model in browsers is so messy, native apps are likely to remain the real interaction sandbox for the near future. Those proprietary environments are where most innovation will happen until standards catch up, which they no doubt eventually will. In the meantime, even with these touch-event headaches, it's worth the effort to make touch and gesture work in the browser. You know the refrain by now: a new medium requires new interactions, and this chapter has tried to show you what they might look like. But designing and building gestures is only half the battle.

Now that you've figured out the gestures for your interface, you have to sort out how people will find them. That's up next.

5

DISCOVERY

HOORAY, YOU HAVE GESTURES! But, um, do your users know it? Gestures are useful only if people can find them. Otherwise, they're Easter eggs, hidden treats for the lucky or determined—and most users are neither. The challenge, of course, is that gestures are invisible, unlike buttons with their labeled invitations to action. If the interface doesn't clearly suggest a gesture, you must help people discover it. This chapter explores the subtle craft of making gestures *seem* intuitive, even when they aren't intrinsically obvious. We'll look for the essentials of self-explanatory UI in sources as varied as magazines, ancient manuscripts, and video games. All demonstrate the gold standard for a discoverable interface: just-in-time education that reveals itself in context, no manual required.

UP-FRONT INSTRUCTIONS ARE NOT THE ANSWER

Designers too often turn to manuals, FAQs, and elaborate cheat-sheet overlays to explain the niceties of three-finger swipes and five-finger pinches. While these guides are valuable ref-

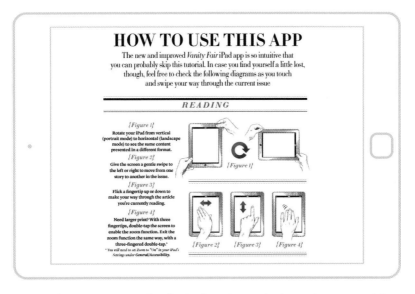

HOW TO USE THIS APP

The new and improved *Vanity Fair* iPad app is so intuitive that you can probably skip this tutorial. In case you find yourself a little lost, though, feel free to check the following diagrams as you touch and swipe your way through the current issue

READING

[Figure 1]
Rotate your iPad from vertical (portrait mode) to horizontal (landscape mode) to see the same content presented in a different format.

[Figure 2]
Give the screen a gentle swipe to the left or right to move from one story to another in the issue.

[Figure 3]
Flick a fingertip up or down to make your way through the article you're currently reading.

[Figure 4]
Need larger print? With three fingertips, double-tap the screen to enable the zoom function. Exit the zoom function the same way, with a three-fingered double-tap.*

* *You will need to set Zoom to "On" in your iPad's Settings under General/Accessibility.*

[Figure 1]

[Figure 2] *[Figure 3]* *[Figure 4]*

FIG 5.1: When *Vanity Fair* introduced an iPad app, its complex instructions suggested the app was anything but the "intuitive" experience they promised.

erences, they're terrible learning tools. When you present too much detail too soon, the result is overwhelming, giving the impression that your app or website is more complicated than it is (**FIG 5.1**).

It isn't only the volume of the instruction that puts people off, it's also that it exists at all. Newcomers to your site or app are there *to get something done,* and instructions feel like a diversion. The rub is that reading them would almost always help us do that thing faster, but we're too impatient to bother. Most of us have incomplete knowledge of the tools that we use every day because we never, *ever* RTFM (read the, ahem, freakin' manual)—which is why strapping a tutorial or video onto the front of your user experience isn't as valuable as letting people dive in and experiment. We'll examine effective onboarding techniques later. But first: sometimes the right interface metaphor is all the instruction people need.

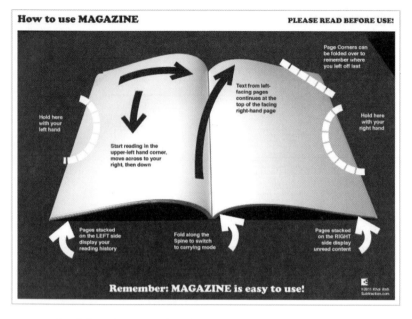

FIG 5.2: What if physical magazines had the same instructions as iPad magazine apps? This sendup by designer Khoi Vinh shows how complicated our most elegant interfaces become when we overload them with instructions.

SKEUOMORPHIC DESIGN: "I ALREADY KNOW HOW TO USE IT"

As we saw in the last chapter, if an interface element looks or behaves like a physical object, people will try to interact with it like one. And the less a gesture resembles a physical action, the harder it is to find. Those guidelines explain the effectiveness of *skeuomorphic design,* an approach that plays dress-up with digital interfaces, making them look (and hopefully act) like physical objects. If an interface looks like a book, it instantly suggests that we should use it like one by swiping through pages to advance through the content. The metaphor teaches simply by matching the visual design to the underlying interaction. *"Hey,*

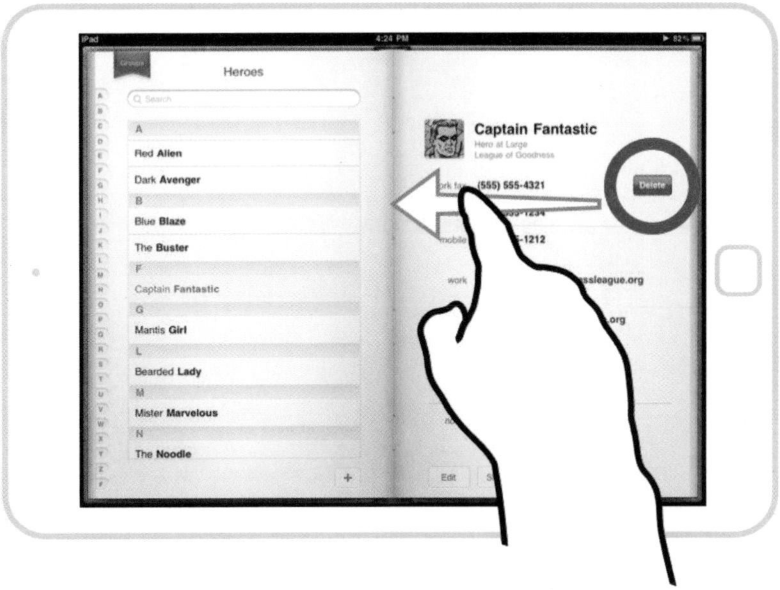

FIG 5.3: The original Contacts app for iPad looked like an address book but didn't act like one. When you swiped to turn the page you instead deleted contact info. Whoops!

that's a knob [or a book or a microphone or a bird-hurling slingshot]. I already know how to use that thing."

Skeuomorphic design runs into trouble as a teaching device, however, when the designer doesn't embrace the metaphor. For the iPad's first eighteen months, the Calendar app's leather-bound datebook didn't behave like a datebook. It looked like the real deal, but when you tried to swipe at its pages, nothing happened. The same was true of the original Contacts app, only worse: swiping the screen to try to turn the address book's pages actually deleted content (**FIG 5.3**).

Such dangerous misdirection shows the damage when visual design doesn't match interaction design. Be aware not only of the interactive opportunities your interface metaphor proposes but the opportunities it *promises*. If your design promises that people can flip pages, then it must allow it. Don't go for "looks like" if you can't pull off "acts like."

FIG 5.4: The designer of this 15th-century Book of Hours drew its pages to make it look like they were written on scrolls of parchment—a playful throwback to an earlier era of reading technology. It's fair to guess that nobody fell for the trick and tried to open the page like a scroll. That changes when you introduce a touchscreen. Image from the Bibliothèques de l'Université de Liège.

The "looks like"–"acts like" pairing at once departs and evolves from what artists and designers have playfully practiced for centuries. Monks etched three-dimensional trompe l'œil effects in illuminated manuscripts to create the illusion of scrolls, curled pages, or stacked sheets of paper (**FIG 5.4**). More recently, interactive designers of the 1980s faithfully reproduced calculators, calendars, and books as UI elements for the Macintosh and other graphical interfaces (**FIG 5.5**). Historically, we've understood these flourishes as ornamentation—harmless eye candy. We didn't expect any direct interaction; we knew that a desktop interface that looked like a book would still be operated via desktop-style buttons. But when that visual prank hits the touchscreen, we're taken in. Remember: the physicality of

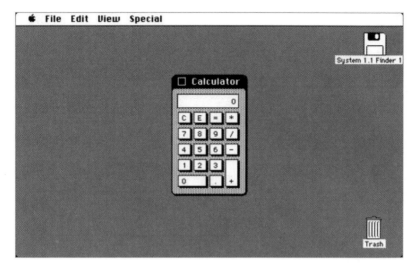

touch creates the illusion that there is no illusion. Touchscreen interfaces that look like physical objects will confuse and misdirect if they don't also act like those objects.

WHEN DESIGN FALLS FLAT

If "looks like" can't travel without "acts like," what about the reverse? Does an interface work if it behaves like a physical element but doesn't look like one? Many designers pooh-pooh the visual aping of real objects for aesthetic reasons, and skeuomorphic design can veer into kitsch. But removing *all* the "looks like" cues for touchscreen elements can flatten more than their looks. iOS provides a cautionary tale.

In 2013, Apple released iOS 7 in a redesign that followed the flat aesthetic popularized by Windows. The company ruthlessly slashed skeuomorphic elements: buttons morphed into unadorned text, sliders became flat blocks, and cards lost their borders and shadows. In doing so, the designers championed a focus on content and visual efficiency, eschewing "frivolous"

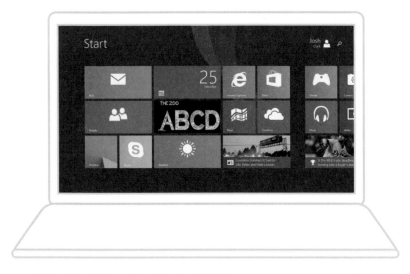

FIG 5.6: The clipped tiles at the right edge of Windows panoramas cue you to swipe or scroll.

decoration like shadows, glossy surfaces, or lighting effects—the trappings of the physical world. Though the goal was worthwhile, the implementation was tough to follow. Experienced Apple users knew how these flattened widgets functioned from past versions, but newcomers faced precious few visual clues. Widgets still behaved with physicality—sliders slid, cards flipped—but figuring out that they were sliders or cards was trial and error. Worse, the flattening of the interface also squashed the discoverability of basic elements, even buttons.

If you eliminate skeuomorphic cues, fill that vacuum with other instructions. They can be subtle suggestions like visual hints or animations. In Windows, the operating system proposes that panoramas, its horizontal tile grids, can be swiped and scrolled by dangling offscreen tiles in partial view (FIG 5.6). In iOS, the "slide to unlock" slider invites swipes by animating a glow from left to right across the text. As for Apple's flat design, the company later retrofitted its operating system with an option to restore a faint outline to its otherwise naked buttons.

These aesthetic interventions and motion cues hint at an element's interactive role, so that it doesn't have to look like an actual object. The sliding tiles in Windows, the list items in the Clear to-do app, the rubber-band bounce in iOS when you reach the end of a list—none of these digital elements pretend to look like a real-world thing, but they do behave according to physics. The illusion of physicality does not rely on things looking real, only acting real. In fact, there's danger in making things look too real.

DON'T BE SO LITERAL

When a design becomes too tied to the physical "truth" of its interface, it risks losing digital opportunities. The magazine industry's first generation of tablet apps, for instance, hewed so closely to the behavior of a paper magazine that they were little more than PDFs. They were dead simple to use—swipe forward and backward—but they didn't take advantage of the most essential digital superpower: random access to content. In many apps, the table of contents was elusive, so you couldn't just leap to the content you wanted to read. The overly literal embrace of the physical metaphor felt like a step backward.

Improve physical metaphors with digital-only enhancements

Let your interfaces do things humdrum physical objects cannot. The innovation of replacing hardware buttons with a touch-screen transformed our devices into shape-shifters, bending the traditional physics of industrial design. At first glance, the *Sydney Morning Herald* iPad app looks and behaves like the paper version. Tap the page-indicator dots at screen bottom, however, and you see a quick-reference list of every headline on that page. Slide your finger across the dots and you scan all the day's stories for instant access to any article without swiping through the whole lot (**FIG 5.7**). The app pairs the familiarity of a paper newspaper with the digital efficiency of unshackling content from an analog page-by-page experience.

FIG 5.7: The *Sydney Morning Herald's* iPad app puts a paged browsing experience front and center, but lets you rapidly browse headlines by sweeping across screen bottom.

The *Herald* app shows that effortless interfaces can draw on more than physical know-how. *Mouse-driven experience informs expectations too.* In Maps for iOS, newcomers easily discover that tapping twice zooms in—something they've gleaned from double-clicking in Google Maps. But you're without a compass when you encounter gestures that have no context or history. Nobody ever fathoms that you can do a two-fingered single tap in iOS Maps to zoom out (that's a real thing). Nothing from either physical or digital maps suggests to even try it. When gestures don't match up with past experience, they become abstract and require explicit help to find.

Explicit help is okay, by the way. I've heard designers say, "If your interface needs explanation, you've failed." It isn't true. While basic features should be easy and obvious from the get-go, advanced features always need a little instruction, even in the most well-considered interface. The best learning takes place while doing, however, which is why help screens and FAQs let us down. A better way is to teach gradually and contextually, and lucky for us, we have a great way to learn how:

PLAY MORE VIDEO GAMES

Video game designers are pros at teaching unfamiliar interfaces. In many games, you don't even know the goal, let alone your capabilities or the obstacles you might encounter. How do you learn this stuff as a player? Not by reading a manual or watching a screencast. *You learn by playing the game.* The game itself teaches you how to play, drawing you in and showing you expert moves once you've mastered the basics. Among other techniques, games lean on three tools to get this done: *coaching, leveling up, and power-ups.*

Coaching

You know the old saw: *telling* how to do something isn't as effective as *showing.* Reading a book is not the best way to learn an instrument or serve a tennis ball. Instead someone shows you, and you imitate and practice. Every modern theory of learning emphasizes the importance of active participation and discovery, supplemented by mentoring. In other words, we learn by doing, and we learn best in the moment. That's coaching, and that's what the best self-teaching interfaces do. Games deploy this approach over and over. Coaching is the game riding along with the player (or your website riding along with the user), demonstrating useful techniques at appropriate moments.

In the iPad version of the game *Dead Space,* the first screen teaches you how to move, applying an overlay that demos what to do, then inviting you to try it yourself (**FIG 5.8**). Once you've traipsed across the room, the overlay disappears. One of the most crucial parts of coaching is knowing when a skill has been learned and when to move on to something new.

FIG 5.8: Learn to walk before you run: an overlay in *Dead Space* provides dead simple coaching to tell you how to move in the first screen of the game. The animated hand traces the cross shape, prompting you to do the same.

FIG 5.9: A simple tutorial for alarm clock app Rise shows static images of the gestures for setting alarms.

FIG 5.10: There's no Continue button in the tutorial for iOS app Mailbox; you have to complete the described gesture to keep moving.

"**Do, don't read" is even better than "show, don't tell.**" *Dead Space* pairs instructions with action; you practice the skill at the same moment it's taught. Compare that to the traditional tutorial that starts so many mobile apps. These tutorials are typically static screens that illustrate key features, controls, or gestures, isolated from the content or actual use of the app (**FIG 5.9**).

Tutorials ask you to commit gestures to visual memory. By making you do an action, *Dead Space* helps you commit the gesture to far more effective muscle memory. Again, the basis of learning physical actions is repetition: a loop of demonstration and practice. When teaching gestures, get people repeating moves early and often. The tutorials for Mailbox (**FIG 5.10**) and Dots (**FIG 5.11**) do just that, forcing you to perform each gesture to continue.

FIG 5.11: The tutorial for the game app *Dots* introduces you to the essential mechanic: connecting dots. To continue the tutorial, you have to complete each dot-connecting task.

Walkthroughs beat tutorials. While the Mailbox and Dots tutorials are effective at teaching controls, they also feel like stilted lessons, a series of hoops to hop through before you can use the app *for real*. *Dead Space* trumps both with its in-context *walkthrough,* a strictly choreographed tour of features in the actual working environment of an app or a site. It's like training wheels: you're moving on your own, but with a few supports to keep you from falling. Note-taking app Noted, for example, guides you through fixed steps for creating and editing your first note (**FIG 5.12**).

Facebook Paper grants you total freedom from a set path; you explore on your own, and Paper explains key interactions as you bump into them (**FIG 5.13**). Gestures are animated onscreen to show you how they work, encouraging you to mimic the motions. (Demonstration and practice!) You can follow the app's cues or not—you stay in control. This is the most effective style of walkthrough, and the kind games most frequently deploy.

All of these coaching examples explain their gestures via text and labels, but you can also hint at features through subtler means, like animation. When the very first *USA Today* app for iPhone was released, it featured a dial at the top of the screen to navigate editorial channels. But many people didn't realize the dial moved and thought the app had only a handful of sections.

FIG 5.12: The walkthrough for Noted takes you on a predetermined path through the app, and you create your first document as you go. The dot animates to show you where to swipe and tap.

FIG 5.13: Paper prompts with animation, text, and speech to explain new features as you find them.

So the designers added an animation: every time you visited the main screen, the dial zipped in from the right (**FIG 5.14**). *"Hey, that moves, maybe I can move it too."* It worked. With the app demonstrating the motion of the control, confusion melted away and visitors swiped the dial as intended. Once you moved the dial yourself, demonstrating you'd learned the trick, the animation stopped running.

FIG 5.14: Adding an animation to *USA Today*'s original dial-style navigation control dramatically improved user awareness of how the thing worked.

Mistakes are a teaching opportunity. Coaching isn't only about observing what people do; it's also what they *fail* to do. Smart teaching layers watch for mistakes and swoop in to offer instruction. Citia is a web-based platform that organizes content into a card format, and you flip cards to the right to motor through a stack of content. If you try to swipe in the wrong direction, the app simultaneously signals the mistake and offers a correction: the card follows the swipe in the "wrong" direction, then bounces back to the correct one. The app honors the user's intent while course-correcting it.

When someone stops interacting, that's another potential sign of trouble—or at least a sign it's not clear to them what to do next. Here again, a gentle animation or other cue helps demonstrate what to do. In the kids' storybook app *The Fantastic Flying Books of Mr. Morris Lessmore,* you get started by swiping open the book's cover (**FIG 5.15**). If you don't after the first several seconds, an animated image appears, telling you to swipe. The best teaching interfaces notice your activity, inactivity, and overall learning progress, and adapt their guidance accordingly. That's where leveling up comes in.

FIG 5.15: When a pause means puzzlement: if you don't swipe to open the book after several seconds on the first screen, a ghostly hand appears to show you what to do.

Leveling up

Don't teach everything at once. Modern education theory advocates teaching in doses, building on the basics and revealing more as the student gets better. Games often do this literally, dividing progress into explicit levels that focus on a new skill. Though most apps and sites aren't as linear as games, the learning curves are similar. Teach the basic interactions first, as people encounter them, before introducing more complex or abstract gestures. (Let people use those advanced gestures if they discover them on their own. Levels aren't about holding people back from new stuff, but rather when you decide to advertise it.)

We're most motivated to pick up a new skill the second we find we need it—like when we run headlong into a terrifying giant wielding an enormous sword. *Infinity Blade* is an iOS game with a wildly sophisticated combat system, but they make it easy to learn by breaking down the elements, teaching one step at a time. Just when you're about to get your head knocked off, the game stops the action in freeze-frame and demonstrates what you need to know to get through the crisis of the moment (**FIG 5.16**).

FIG 5.16: One skill at a time: *Infinity Blade* pauses at incredibly convenient times to offer training on a specific ability. Once you've mastered blocking (top) you're ready to tackle dodging, etc.

Again, the emphasis is on demonstration and practice. The game shows you the gesture or control to use and then waits for you; when you use the new gesture, the action continues... *and your first interaction is a success.* When an interaction is important enough, it's okay to pause and force people to try the gesture to continue.

Apple used this approach when it introduced OSX Lion, a software update that changed how scrolling works. They turned virtual gravity upside down, so that the mouse or trackpad moved in the reverse direction to what Mac users were accustomed to for decades. To teach this gesture, Apple showed a dialog box right when you installed the software, explaining what was different and inviting you to try scrolling to test it out. In fact, *you had to scroll* because that was the only way to get to the Continue button. Scroll, click the button, and BOOM: you just beat level one of Apple's operating system.

Now you're ready to try it out on your own; continue using your new skill in the current "level" until you encounter a fresh challenge and need fresh training. Think about your app as levels. You want to motivate and enable people to move from novice to expert to master. How do you teach the basics and, once that's done, the advanced maneuvers? Too often we treat our apps and websites as just one level. We do a quick introduction and then release our users into the cold wilderness of our software. Embracing the concept of leveling up means you follow and teach people throughout their journey to mastery. And every so often, you should reward them for their progress.

Power-ups

In games, as you get better, you earn power-ups, little turbo-boosts to your play through some extra speed or special ability. If gestures are the shortcuts of touch, then power-ups are the shortcuts of video games—usable by anyone but especially efficient in the hands of an expert. They not only unlock new abilities but they're also rewards, markers of your progress as you move through the game's levels. Teaching an advanced or abstract gesture is like delivering a power-up, and it gives users a similar thrill of satisfaction.

When Twitter overhauled its iPhone app in late 2011, they missed a power-up opportunity to reveal an abstract gesture. The redesign moved access to direct messages (DMs) off of the main navigation, burying them a level deeper in the Me tab. For heavy DM users, that meant two taps every time they wanted to check direct messages. To ease this burden, Twitter helpfully provided a gesture for quicker access: swipe up from the Me tab to go directly to your messages. Trouble is, they never told anyone about it, so most people didn't know the option existed.

It's useful to let people learn the slow way before you teach shortcuts. In Twitter's case, learning to tap the Me tab and then the Direct Messages button reinforced the app's mental model, teaching people where DMs lived. But after doing that five or ten times, you've demonstrated that you've learned the route. What the interface *should* have done at that point is dispense a power-up—unveiling the gesture shortcut with an animated demonstration, and then requiring you to copy the gesture to move on (**FIG 5.17**).

FIG 5.17: This simple mock-up shows how Twitter could have improved discovery of its Direct Messages gesture shortcut. After tapping the DM button ten times, the app should have shown an instructional message with a gesture animation.

It might seem silly, but it's true: there's delight in learning a new skill like this, of being told a secret. The fun of video games is in the rush of getting better, of advancing the storyline. With more mundane apps, that storyline is the user's work or career, and the reward in these advanced gestures and shortcuts is nothing less than becoming more awesome at what they do. Think like a game designer, and you'll deliver the same endorphin boost to your "players." A great discoverability strategy feels like a prize, not an instruction.

WE'RE JUST GETTING STARTED

The need to teach gestures in the first place only points up the fact that we don't yet have many established standards. That makes this both an exciting and overwhelming time for designers and consumers alike. As designers, we need to talk to each other, examine each other's work, share ideas for gestural conventions, and commit to codifying them. We have our own coaching and leveling up to do here.

Our job is getting harder. We have to design for a ton of platforms and, in doing so, juggle endless varieties of input methods. But difficult challenges often disguise remarkable opportunities. We have the chance right now to invent more humane ways to interact with information. In part, it's a moment for study, for refining our technical know-how (44-pixel touch targets!). But perhaps more urgently, it's also a moment to step back from crufty best practices and allow ourselves to imagine fresh possibilities in this developing medium. Take hold of your touchscreens, think big, and go make something amazing.

Inspiration from industrial design

Much of this book has focused on the physical aspects of touch design, drawing connections to the centuries of industrial design that preceded the touchscreen. The following books offer a useful grounding in that tradition:

- *Designing for People,* Henry Dreyfuss. Considered the founder of modern industrial design, Dreyfuss designed the Bell telephone, the Honeywell thermostat, the Hoover vacuum cleaner, and other classics of twentieth-century design. His touchstone book from 1955 remains as fresh as ever.
- *The Design of Everyday Things,* Don Norman. A fun and enlightening romp through our designed environment, this essential book points out why the designs of physical objects work well (and why they don't).
- *Designing Devices,* Dan Saffer. This brief ebook explores the elements that have defined great device interfaces since the ancient world.

Human factors and the touchscreen

The field of human factors focuses on fitting technology neatly within the capabilities and limitations of the human body. It boils down to comfort—designing interfaces that are physically and cognitively easy to master. These resources address the human factors of touch:

- "Multi-touch Systems That I Have Known and Loved," Bill Buxton. A wonderful off-the-cuff treatise on the good and bad of touch design, from a UX trailblazer who also co-invented the capacitive touchscreen (http://bkaprt.com/dft/06-01/).
- "How Do Users Really Hold Mobile Devices?," Steven Hoober. Focuses on the ergonomics and accuracy of various smartphone grips (http://bkaprt.com/dft/01-03/).

- **"Making Learning Usable: How We Use Mobile Devices,"** Steven Hoober and Patti Shank. Extends Hoober's previous study to tablets and phablets (http://bkaprt.com/dft/01-07/).
- **"Designing for a Thumb: An Ideal Mobile Touchscreen Interface for Chinese Users,"** Qian Fei. A careful analysis of thumb accuracy on mobile touchscreens, positing the fan-shaped thumb zone for smartphones (http://bkaprt.com/dft/01-04/).
- **"User Learning and Performance with Marking Menus,"** Gordon Kurtenbach and Bill Buxton. The dramatic speed increases of gesture-based radial menus versus traditional linear menus (http://bkaprt.com/dft/04-05/).

Platform design guidelines

Each platform has its own specific rules. Dig into the design guidelines for each of the popular touch operating systems:

- **iOS Human Interface Guidelines.** Apple's worldview of good experiences on iPhone and iPad, from high-level design principles to detailed use of individual controls (http://bkaprt.com/dft/06-02/).
- **Material Design.** The visual language that Google uses across all platforms, including Android; this site explains its philosophy and implementation details (http://bkaprt.com/dft/06-03/).
- **Windows Design.** Guidelines for creating Windows 10 apps on devices from phones to jumbo-screen computers (http://bkaprt.com/dft/06-04/).

Smartwatch guidelines

This book's general touch guidelines apply to the new crop of smartwatches, too, but with a few constraints. Apple and Google provide their respective specifics.

- **Apple Watch Human Interface Guidelines** (http://bkaprt.com/dft/06-05/)
- **Android Wear** (http://bkaprt.com/dft/06-06/)

Coding gestures for the web

- **"Multi-touch Web Development,"** Boris Smus. Introduces the techniques (and pitfalls) of coding gestures with touch events (http://bkaprt.com/dft/04-11/).
- **"Touch and Mouse,"** Chris Wilson and Paul Kinlan. How to code interactions that work well with both touch and cursor interfaces (http://bkaprt.com/dft/06-07/).
- **"Unifying Touch and Mouse: How Pointer Events Will Make Cross-Browsers Touch Support Easy,"** David Rousset. Coding pointer events for cross-browser compatibility (http://bkaprt.com/dft/06-08/).

A handful of JavaScript libraries helps reduce the significant agony of coding gestures for the web by abstracting the differences among mouse, touch, and pointer events:

- **Hammer.js.** Detects several gestures in modern browsers (including IE 9+): tap, double-tap, long press, swipe, pinch, and rotate (http://bkaprt.com/dft/06-09/).
- **Hand.js.** A polyfill library from Microsoft that lets you use pointer events in all browsers (http://bkaprt.com/dft/04-16/).
- **Tappy,** Filament Group's Scott Jehl. Papers over the differences among touch, mouse, and keyboard click events by creating a single tap event that works for all three (http://bkaprt.com/dft/04-14/).

Touch notation tools

Pen and paper are my best planning tools. I always start there, writing out ideas in longhand and then shifting to loose sketches of screens and widgets. This toolkit has one big drawback, though: it doesn't move. That makes representing the motion of gestures challenging. Several smarties have come to my rescue, however, with detailed notations for representing touch gestures:

- **"Touch Notation,"** Matt Gemmell. A simple system for representing complex gestures (http://bkaprt.com/dft/06-10/).
- **Cue,** P.J. Onori. A set of compact gesture icons available in SVG, PNG, OmniGraffle, and InDesign formats, for use in wireframes and other documentation (http://bkaprt.com/dft/06-11/).
- **Touchscreen stencils.** Dan Saffer and Rachel Glaves. A set of drawings of hands performing common gestures, available in loads of digital formats. These stencils provide clear, literal representations of each gesture (http://bkaprt.com/dft/06-12/).

It's confounding that my name is alone on the cover when so many made this book go. Very special thanks to my partner in this fandango, my marvelous editor Tina Lee, who revealed the book that lurked inside a mass of ideas. She untangled my prose, helped me find paths (and connect them) when I got lost, and quieted a snarling collection of writing quirks I never even knew existed. Like Tina, A Book Apart's Katel LeDû patiently kept me on track with a hand that was sometimes stern but more often generous with high fives.

Thanks to Mandy Brown for encouraging me to start writing this book, to Jeffrey Zeldman for encouraging me to keep at it, and to Jason Santa Maria and Rob Weychert for making it look so kick-ass. Thanks to Caren Litherland for her sharpshooter targeting of errant punctuation and clumsy grammar.

The ideas in this book were developed and tested during the design of many websites and apps. Dull notions became sharp design principles thanks to the steel of my frequent collaborators, who prove the rule that you should always work with people smarter than you. Among them, special thanks to my confederate Brad Frost, who also penned the foreword for this book (thus laying claim to several touchscreen puns before I could use them myself). Thanks to my coconspirators Dan Mall, Jennifer Brook, TJ Pitre, Jonathan Stark, Ethan Marcotte, Kevin Hoffman, Melissa Frost, Kelli Shaver, Robert Gorell, Robert Jolly, and Kristina Frantz. Thanks, too, to my clients, who were game to push the frontier with us and try new techniques. From the project archives, special shouts to Abby McInerney, Teri Everett, and David Fine for Time Inc.; Sara Winge and Edie Freedman for O'Reilly Media; Chad Schlegel and Bill Gannon for *Entertainment Weekly;* Tony Brancato for *People Magazine;* Ned Desmond and Christine Ying for *TechCrunch;* Cathy Ferrara for Scholastic; and Samantha Katz, Joel Smernoff, and Peter Meyers for Citia.

I have the rare fortune to be friends with people who are also my heroes. I often pinch myself at the company I'm in, even more so that they're all so generous with their ideas and suggestions. My fellow traveler Luke Wroblewski never fails to make me smarter about mobile, especially over late-night drinks. He also convened the Mobilewood crew, whose future-friendly influence is reflected throughout this book. Thanks to the mighty Mobilewood brains of Brad Frost (again), Lyza Danger Gardner, Jason Grigsby, Scott Jehl, Scott Jenson, Tim Kadlec, Jeremy Keith, Brian LeRoux, Bryan Rieger, Stephanie Rieger, and Andrea Trasatti. Thanks to my Providence crew: Jennifer Robbins, Jason Pamental, Bil Herron, and Coryndon Luxmoore for reality-checking my early notions on touchscreen design. I'm grateful for expansive conversations with my smart friends Rachel Hinman, David VanEsselstyn, Carla Diana, Rusty Mitchell, Loren Brichter, John Gruber, and my hacking partner (and Brooklyn's sweetheart), Larry Legend. Thanks, too, to Bill Buxton for his encouraging words and to Steven Hoober and Patti Shank for their tireless mobile research efforts.

My gumption is goosed daily by the enthusiasm and creativity of my studiomates in Brooklyn. Thanks to all of you and especially to Swissmiss Tina Roth Eisenberg for creating a remarkable community at Friends, and to Jessi Arrington and Creighton Mershon for filling Studiomates with so much spirit (and color!).

Finally, I'm so very grateful to the two loves of my life: my wife, Liza, and our daughter, Nika. Nika's boundless optimism and wonder constantly replenish my own, and her always inventive uses of phones and tablets remind me that we've only begun to scratch the surface of how we'll interact with information—and one another. And holy cats, Liza, you make everything possible. Every day you teach me, challenge me, encourage me, thrill me. You help me be the best Josh Clark I can be, and you've certainly made me the luckiest man alive. Thank you for sharing this wonderful life with me.

REFERENCES

Shortened URLs are numbered sequentially; the related long URLs are listed below for reference.

Introduction

00-01 http://www.pewinternet.org/2015/04/01/us-smartphone-use-in-2015
00-02 http://www.cnbc.com/id/39501308
00-03 http://pewinternet.org/Reports/2014/E-Reading-Update/Tablet-and-Ereader-Ownership/Half-of-American-adults-now-own-a-tablet-or-ereader.aspx

00-04 http://www.asymco.com/2012/02/16/ios-devices-in-2011-vs-macs-sold-it-in-28-years

Chapter 1

01-01 https://archive.org/details/bstj39-4-995
01-02 http://www.tecmark.co.uk/smartphone-usage-data-uk-2014/
01-03 http://www.uxmatters.com/mt/archives/2013/02/how-do-users-really-hold-mobile-devices.php

01-04 http://link.springer.com/chapter/10.1007/978-3-642-39241-2_6
01-05 http://www.cmo.com/content/dam/CMO_Other/ADI/ADI_Mobile_Report_2014/2014_US_Mobile_Benchmark_Report.pdf

01-06 http://samsungtomorrow.com/사용자의-눈과-손에-딱-맞는-대화면-갤럭시-w-출시

01-07 http://www.elearningguild.com/research/archives/index.cfm?id=174&action=viewonly

01-08 http://www.sfgate.com/news/article/Steve-Jobs-Touchscreen-Laptops-Don-t-Work-AAPL-2477126.php

01-09 http://www.intelfreepress.com/news/do-people-want-touch-on-laptop-screens/

01-10 http://www.sciencedirect.com/science/article/pii/S1057740813000934
01-11 http://www.slideshare.net/uxpa-dc/the-hybrids-are-coming-john-whalen
01-12 https://www.flickr.com/photos/intelfreepress/6837427202
01-13 https://www.flickr.com/photos/intelfreepress/6983554875
01-14 http://www.abookapart.com/products/mobile-first
01-15 http://thesession.org

01-16 http://www.google.com/design/spec/components/buttons.html# buttons-floating-action-button

01-17 https://www.flickr.com/photos/janitors/10065590424

01-18 http://www.apple.com/

Chapter 2

02-01 http://dev.w3.org/csswg/mediaqueries-4/#pointer

02-02 https://www.usertesting.com

02-03 http://www.w3.org/WAI/GL/css2em.htm

02-04 http://mobile-ux.appspot.com/#8

02-05 http://go.microsoft.com/fwlink/p/?linkid=242592

02-06 https://msdn.microsoft.com/en-us/library/windows/desktop/ Dn742468(v=VS.85).aspx

02-07 https://instagram.com/p/q89q9djBkq/

Chapter 3

03-01 http://www.mcwade.com/DesignTalk/2013/09/flat-is-cool-but-be-consistent

03-02 http://www.lukew.com/ff/entry.asp?1569

03-03 http://erikrunyon.com/2013/01/carousel-stats/

03-04 http://www.nngroup.com/articles/auto-forwarding/

03-05 http://yorkwebteam.blogspot.com/2013/03/are-homepage-carousels-effective-aka.html

03-06 http://shouldiuseacarousel.com

03-07 http://www.statista.com/statistics/232285/reasons-for-online-shopping-cart-abandonment

03-08 http://blog.hubspot.com/blog/tabid/6307/bid/6746/Which-Types-of-Form-Fields-Lower-Landing-Page-Conversions.aspx

03-09 http://zdfs.github.io/toscani/paymentInfo

03-10 http://blogs.forrester.com/michael_ogrady/12-06-19-sms_usage_remains_strong_in_the_us_6_billion_sms_messages_are_sent_each_day

03-11 http://www.pewinternet.org/2012/03/19/teens-smartphones-texting

03-12 http://leaverou.github.io/awesomplete/

03-13 https://github.com/miketaylr/jquery.datalist.js

03-14 http://www.wsj.com/articles/SB10001424127887323566804578549351972 660468

03-15   http://bits.blogs.nytimes.com/2013/09/29/disruptions-guided-by-touch-screens-blind-turn-to-smartphones-for-sight

03-16   https://www.youtube.com/watch?v=h2OfQdYrHRs

03-17   http://www.w3.org/TR/webaudio

03-18   http://dvcs.w3.org/hg/speech-api/raw-file/tip/speechapi.html

03-19   http://www.w3.org/TR/geolocation-API

03-20   http://w3c.github.io/deviceorientation/spec-source-orientation.html

03-21   http://www.w3.org/TR/ambient-light

Chapter 4

04-01   https://www.flickr.com/photos/jking89/4572668303

04-02   https://www.flickr.com/photos/blackcountrymuseums/4385115536

04-03   http://www.chicagomanualofstyle.org/tools_proof.html

04-04   http://www.donhopkins.com/drupal/node/100

04-05   http://www.billbuxton.com/MMUserLearn.html

04-06   http://tikku.com/jquery-radmenu-plugin

04-07   http://lab.victorcoulon.fr/css/path-menu

04-08   https://github.com/filamentgroup/Overthrow

04-09   https://drafts.csswg.org/css-snappoints/

04-10   http://www.w3.org/TR/touch-events/

04-11   http://www.html5rocks.com/en/mobile/touch

04-12   https://msdn.microsoft.com/en-us/library/windows/apps/Hh767313.aspx

04-13   https://github.com/ftlabs/fastclick

04-14   https://github.com/filamentgroup/tappy

04-15   http://www.w3.org/TR/pointerevents/

04-16   http://handjs.codeplex.com

04-17   https://msdn.microsoft.com/library/dn433244.aspx

Resources

06-01   http://www.billbuxton.com/multitouchOverview.html

06-02   https://developer.apple.com/library/ios/documentation/UserExperience/Conceptual/MobileHIG

06-03   https://www.google.com/design/spec/material-design/introduction.html

06-04   https://dev.windows.com/en-us/design

06-06   https://developer.apple.com/watch/human-interface-guidelines

06-07   http://www.html5rocks.com/en/mobile/touchandmouse

06-08 http://blogs.msdn.com/b/davrous/archive/2015/08/10/handling-touch-in-your-html5-apps-thanks-to-the-pointer-events-of-ie10-and-windows-8.aspx

06-09 http://hammerjs.github.io

06-10 http://mattgemmell.com/touch-notation

06-11 http://somerandomdude.com/work/cue

06-12 http://www.kickerstudio.com/2008/12/touchscreen-stencils

INDEX

ABOUT A BOOK APART

We cover the emerging and essential topics in web design and development with style, clarity, and above all, brevity—because working designer-developers can't afford to waste time.

COLOPHON

The text is set in FF Yoga and its companion, FF Yoga Sans, both by Xavier Dupré. Headlines and cover are set in Titling Gothic by David Berlow.

 This book was printed in the United States using FSC certified Finch papers.